A SIMPLE GUIDE
TO RETIREMENT

A SIMPLE GUIDE TO RETIREMENT

How to Make Retirement Work for You

Morley D. Glicken and Brian Haas

PRAEGER
An Imprint of ABC-CLIO, LLC

A B C ⬥ C L I O

Santa Barbara, California • Denver, Colorado • Oxford, England

Library of Congress Cataloging-in-Publication Data

Glicken, Morley D.

A simple guide to retirement : how to make retirement work for you / by Morley D. Glicken and Brian Haas.

p. cm.

Includes index.

ISBN 978-0-313-37229-2 (hard copy : alk. paper)

1. Retirement—Planning. I. Haas, Brian. II. Title.

HQ1062.G55   2009

646.7′9—dc22   2009009904

13 12 11 10 9 1 2 3 4 5

This book is also available on the World Wide Web as an eBook.

Visit www.abc-clio.com for details.

ABC-CLIO, LLC
130 Cremona Drive, P.O. Box 1911
Santa Barbara, California 93116-1911

This book is printed on acid-free paper ∞

Manufactured in the United States of America

Contents

Preface

Retirement is a serious event in anyone's life, particularly in perilous economic times. It deserves better than the homilies, folk wisdom, and aphorisms you'll find in many books on the subject. Because economic times are changing quickly, you deserve to know about retirement from the best available research and to have an accurate view of the future so the decisions you make will be based on best evidence and not on someone's subjective opinion.

In the following chapters, we intend to give you the best research-guided information available so you can make retirement decisions early enough in your life that, when the time comes to actually retire, you'll do it in a rational way that will ensure the best possible results. For those of you who are close to retirement, there is helpful information to guide you through the process. And for those of you who are retired but find retirement less than a happy experience, we have a lot of good research to share with you as well. We're serious people, and this is a serious subject and book.

We intend to provide information that will help you with all the decisions you will make as you work toward retirement, including where to live, financial decisions so you have sufficient savings to retire gracefully, health-related issues to consider, how you know you're ready to retire, what to do to test the waters to see if you really are ready, and how to handle the additional time you'll have once you stop working full time. Some thoughtful people have looked at each of these issues. Our goal in this book is to share that information with you. An informed reader is best equipped to make successful decisions.

I (Morley Glicken) am a 68-year-old social work professor and writer. I know a lot about the social and emotional aspects of retirement because I've been there and I've gone through the many contradictory emotions of retiring, un-retiring, and finally having a mix of work and leisure activities that give me great pleasure. I write about those issues and issues related to health care, single life, family involvement in retirement decisions, and finding the best place to live if you plan to move. Brian Haas writes about the money aspects of retirement including having a nest egg, how to get one that grows well beyond the cost of living, and understanding pension plans and Social Security. He runs a very successful equity fund and helps clients with early financial planning. Between the two of us, we intend to give you the best information we can to help you make informed decisions. Retirement is about the last third of your life. You deserve to approach it with the same thoughtful preparation you've used in developing the first two-thirds of your life.

Morley D. Glicken, DSW
Brian Haas, MS

Part I

ATTITUDES TOWARD RETIREMENT

Chapters 1 and 2 discuss the way people view retirement before and after they retire. You'll be surprised (maybe not) that people have serious concerns about the way retirement will affect them but usually find that the reality is much more positive. Most people thrive after they retire. Certainly, the tough economic times we're in create a good deal of realistic anxiety about finances. But in many other ways, retirement satisfaction is very high—good news for those of you who are going through the retirement planning process.

1 ▪ ▪ ▪

Are You Ready to Retire?

We promised a book heavy in research findings on every significant aspect of retirement. This is a good place to start. This chapter considers the research on how people think about retirement while they are still working and the reality after they've retired.

▪ Attitudes about Retirement

How do older people anticipate the ways in which retirement will affect their lives, and how retirement will differ from their working lives? Brougham and Walsh (2005) asked more than 250 employees of a large university who varied in age from 55 to 77 to indicate the relative importance of 29 goals and whether retirement or continued work would achieve those goals. This is important because it indicates a set of beliefs about what will happen to people after they retire. People in the study who were still working believed the following would take place after they retired:

1. Achievement would decline from 54 percent to 27 percent.
2. Contribution to the community and to the greater society would decline from 40 percent to 28 percent.

3. Creativity would increase from 21 percent to 47 percent. This might suggest that jobs are currently thought of as uncreative or that people in the survey believed they'd have more time for hobbies and other creative endeavors. The researchers defined creativity as being curious, wanting to learn, and having original and novel ideas.
4. The quality of their family lives would improve from 33 percent to 48 percent.
5. Freedom would increase from 33 percent to 68 percent.
6. Finances would decrease from 84 percent to 16 percent. The researchers defined finances as the ability to maintain a comfortable standard of living and having sufficient financial reserves to provide for self and family (e.g., money for a college education for children/ grandchildren, emergencies, health insurance, etc.). We'll have a good deal more to say about financial health in future chapters, but clearly a large majority of workers believed they'd be in much worse financial shape after they retired. How about you? What do you think?
7. Stress would increase from 28 percent to 41 percent. The researchers included the words *failure* and *guilt* in defining stress. It's possible that the subjects believed they'd feel guilty about not working and that the loss of work would leave them with less status.
8. Marriages would improve from 31 percent to 48 percent.
9. Social life and self-reliance would all decrease from high 50 percent to low 30 percent.
10. Work opportunities would decrease from 81 percent to only 8 percent. The researchers defined work opportunities as including having a rewarding job that also provided interaction with others. Clearly, this group of workers believed that their social network would diminish with retirement and that satisfying work would be difficult to find.
11. Intellectual functioning would decline from 58 percent to 35 percent. The researchers defined intellectual functioning as participation in activities that stimulated the mind and provided an opportunity to learn new skills, which could be applied to a different career. The subjects must have believed that retirement would limit their motivation to learn, and that without a job new skills would not develop.

◼ The Actual Satisfaction with Retirement

Overall satisfaction with retirement

Smith and Moen (2004) found that 79 percent of more than 400 retirees they sampled said they were satisfied with their lives as retirees. The

Health and Retirement Study (2003), with more than 18,000 subjects, found that 62 percent had high levels of satisfaction with retirement, while 33 percent said they were only somewhat satisfied, and only 5 percent reported dissatisfaction. The same study found that health affected retirement satisfaction, as one might expect, and that, not surprisingly, people who left jobs or careers on good terms were more satisfied with retirement than those who didn't. A 2002 national study by the Rand Corporation found that:

1. Most people say they are not only satisfied but "very satisfied" with retirement. In particular, people in better health and with more financial resources tend to be more satisfied (p. 15).
2. Retirees who can pay for more of their retirement expenses from life-long guaranteed pensions (vs. accumulated savings) are more satisfied (p. 16).
3. Retirees who have received some retirement planning education, or have a financial advisor, or have purchased long-term care insurance are more satisfied than those who have not (p. 17).

Marriage satisfaction

When couples were asked about their satisfaction with retirement, 67 percent of the individual spouses said they were satisfied with retirement, while 59 percent of the couples surveyed said they were jointly satisfied, according to a study by Smith and Moen (2004) of more than 400 retirees aged 50–72. Those couples most likely to report being satisfied with retirement, individually and jointly, were those retired wives and their husbands whose wives reported that their husbands were not influential in their retirement decision. When a spouse retired and the other spouse was expected to stop work and move to a new locale as part of the overall retirement plan, satisfaction with retirement decreased, as did, one could assume, marital satisfaction.

Stress and mental health

Drentea (2002) analyzed data from two large national studies of retirement satisfaction with thousands of subjects. She concluded that retirement actually improves mental health because it decreases anxiety and distress often associated with work. However, there is also evidence that working increases one's sense of control and ability to problem solve, important activities for good mental health. The important finding here is that researchers thought they would find that stress increased in the study sited earlier (Brougham and Walsh, 2005), but it actually decreased in studies of retirees. Another important finding is that as much as people associate retirement with depression, the study found that depression actually decreased with retirement. Bakalar (2006) reports on a study of 280 socially disadvantaged men with low-level jobs who were interviewed about life satisfaction from adolescence until an average age of 75. The researchers found that happiness in retirement didn't depend on good health or having a large income in this group of men. Men who found retirement satisfying were more than twice as likely to report enjoying relationships, volunteering, and having hobbies among their favorite activities, as were those who found retirement unrewarding. Men who were unhappily retired said that they occupied their lives with what the researchers called "autistic activities" such as watching television, gambling, or caring for themselves. For example, 43 percent of the happiest retirees said they found purpose in community service, while only 7 percent of those who found retirement unsatisfying did so. The researchers concluded that many of the issues that contribute to satisfaction after retirement are quite different from those that assure a contented and economically secure middle age.

Satisfaction with finances

We will have much more to say about finances in the next few chapters, but the financial landscape for retirees has changed dramatically because of the burst of the real estate bubble, much higher energy costs, increases in the cost of living, and higher costs associated with health care. Some signs of things to come are found in several recent events:

Bankruptcies

Bankruptcies among older adults have increased. Dugas (2008) notes that from 1991 to 2007, the rate of personal bankruptcy filings among those aged 65 or older jumped by 150 percent, according to the American Association of Retired Persons (AARP). The most startling rise occurred among those aged 75 to 84, whose rate soared 433 percent. Dugas writes, "Now, instead of going into retirement loaded with assets, Americans are hitting their retirement years loaded with debt" (p. 13c). For the elderly, bankruptcy is a particular concern because it's typically harder for seniors, usually lacking in well-paying job opportunities, to climb back out of it.

A sinking stock market

As the stock market tries to adjust to higher costs and the sub-prime housing troubles reduce the worth of homes, many older adults are seeing their savings diminish. For example, Stern (2008) writes that an individual with a $500,000 portfolio who experiences a 15 percent market decline in a year, and also withdraws 7 percent of his portfolio, may deplete the portfolio to $390,000 at the end of the first year. This requires a whopping

28 percent return just to break even at the end of the second year. One can see how this will make it likely that older adults who thought they were financially secure may find their net worth considerably reduced in a short period of time.

Social satisfaction

Prince et al. (1997) (p. 326) found that available studies of adults over age 65 indicate that 5–15 percent reported frequently feeling lonely, and an additional 20–40 percent reported occasional feelings of loneliness. However, 50 percent of adults over age 80 often feel lonely. Sorkin and colleagues (2002) found that social isolation and loneliness compromised immune functioning and have been linked to cardiovascular disease and depression. Gellene (February 10, 2007) reported a study done at Rush Medical Center in Chicago, which found that loneliness often precedes dementia in subjects over age 80. The study found that the risk of dementia increased 51 percent for every one-point increase on a five-point scale of loneliness. The same study found that in men and women aged 50–67, subjects who rated themselves as very lonely had blood pressure readings fully 30 points higher than subjects in the study who didn't rate themselves as being lonely. Although rates of loneliness among older adults might be higher than in other age groups because of the death of loved ones and health problems, loneliness is a problem for older adults who were either lonely before they retired or who find that the loss of work reduces their network of friendships. This may be even truer among those who relocate after retirement and find it difficult to make friends.

A number of writers are concerned that many of us are lonely regardless of age. Robert Putnam (Stossel, 2000) believes that America is developing into a country without a sense of social connectedness where "supper eaten with friends or family has given way to supper gobbled in solitude, with only the glow of the television screen for companionship" (p. 1). According to Putnam, "Americans today have retreated into isolation. Evidence shows that fewer and fewer contemporary Americans are unionizing, voting, rallying around shared causes, participating in religious services, inviting each other over, or doing much of anything collectively. In fact, when we do occasionally gather—for twelve-step support encounters and the like—it's most often only as an excuse to focus on ourselves in the presence of an audience" (Stossel, 2000, p. 1).

Putnam believes that the lack of social involvement negatively affects health, reduces tax responsibilities and charitable work, decreases productivity and "even simple human happiness—all are demonstrably affected by how (and whether) we connect with our family and friends and neighbors and co-workers" (Stossel, 2000, p. 1). Concerns about loneliness often accompany thoughts about retirement, particularly among single people.

We'll have much more to say about loneliness in a chapter on mental health, and another on being single and retired, particularly ways in which one can cope effectively with loneliness before and after one retires.

Satisfaction with health

In a study of satisfaction with health, Vaillant and Mukamal (2001) found that elderly people taking three to eight medications a day who were seen as chronically ill by their physicians saw themselves as healthier than their peers. A person's positive view of life can have a significant impact on the way people perceive their physical and emotional health. This is strongly supported by a study of the physical and emotional health among a Catholic order of women in the Midwest (Danner, Snowdon, and Friesen, 2001). The study found that the personal statements written by very young women to enter the religious order predicted how long they would live. The more positive and affirming the personal statements written when applicants were in their late teens and early twenties, the longer their life spans, sometimes as long as 10 years beyond the mean length of life for the religious order, and up to 20 years or more longer than the general population. Many of the women in the sample lived well into their nineties, and beyond. Of the 650 women in the study, six were over 100 years of age. While some of the women in the sample suffered from serious physical problems, including dementia and Alzheimer's, the numbers were much smaller than in the general population and the age of onset was usually much later in life. The reasons for increased life span in this population seems to be related to good health practices (the order doesn't permit liquor or smoking, and foods are often fresh with a focus on vegetables), and an environment that focuses on spiritual issues and helping others. The order also has a strong emphasis on maintaining a close, supportive relationship among its members, so when illness does arise, there is a network of positive and supportive help.

In a further indication that optimism is the key to whether one is satisfied with health, Jeste (2005) and her colleagues studied more than 500 older Americans, aged 60 to 98, who lived independently within the community (i.e., did not live in a nursing home or assisted care facility). Participants were asked to complete a questionnaire including medical, psychological, and demographic information. The sample was representative of national averages with regard to incidences of medical conditions (e.g., heart disease, cancer, diabetes, etc.). Similarly, 20–25 percent of the respondents had been diagnosed with and/or received treatment for a mental health problem. Despite the prevalence of physical illness and disabilities in the group, when participants in the study were asked to rate their own degree of successful aging on a 10-point scale (with 10 being "most successful"), their average rating was 8.4 (p. 27).

■ What These Findings Tell Us

Are people satisfied with life after they retire? For the most part, yes, but what does satisfaction mean? Generally it's about perception—that is, life may be awful, but if you perceive it as good or as good as it can be, you're likely to say you're satisfied. Researchers talk about social desirability when responding to questions about happiness—that is, people tend to respond in a more positive way because doing so makes them look more successful and happy. With that in mind, let's look briefly at what researchers think contributes to happiness after retirement.

Vaillant and Mukamal (2001) found the following: (a) Elderly adults who age successfully have the ability to plan ahead and are still intellectually curious and in touch with their creative abilities; (b) successfully aging adults, even those over 95, see life as being meaningful and are able to use humor in their daily lives; (c) aging successfully includes remaining physically active and continuing with activities (e.g., walking) that were engaged in at an earlier age in order to remain healthy; (d) older adults who age successfully are more serene and spiritual in their outlook on life than those who age less well; and (e) successful aging includes concern for continued friendships, positive interpersonal relationships, satisfaction with loved ones and family life, and social responsibility in the form of volunteer work and civic involvement. The best evidence is that satisfaction as we age is a combination of good health practices that maintain physical health, continued friendships and family interaction, a positive involvement with hobbies and volunteerism, community, work, and a continued desire to learn and grow intellectually.

■ Rating Your Own Attitudes toward Retirement

Now let us ask you to rate your own attitudes toward retirement honestly by answering the following questions, some of which were raised at the beginning of the chapter. If you've already retired, that's fine, since you can use the questions to measure your current satisfaction with retirement. Answer each question on a 1–10 scale, with 10 being the best you can be and 1 the worst. The questions pertain to what *you* think your life will be like after you retire (or for those who are retired, what life is like at present). After you answer the questions, we'll tell you what your answers mean.

1. Your level of achievement after you retire: 1–10
2. Your happiness with family life: 1–10
3. Your happiness with your marriage: 1–10
4. How happy your spouse will be after you retire: 1–10
5. How well you'll use your free time: 1–10

6. The likeliness that you'll travel: 1–10
7. Your finances: 1–10
8. Your physical health: 1–10
9. Your level of stress: 1–10
10. Your social life: 1–10
11. Your interest in developing new career opportunities: 1–10
12. Your interest in hobbies: 1–10
13. Your willingness to volunteer: 1–10
14. Your level of exercise and sports activity: 1–10
15. Your willingness to continue learning: 1–10.

What Your Score Means

The total number of points you can get is 150. We think that you need a score of at least 120 to have a positive attitude toward your life after you retire. That's an average score of at least eight for each question. Some questions are more powerful than others. Having enough finances to retire comfortably is a very important issue. If you've scored that question very low, it signals that you have concerns about retirement and whether you can afford it at this point. You may change your mind after reading future chapters on finances. If you score well below 120, you're obviously ambivalent about retirement, or you have some concerns that you need to resolve. At the end of the book, we'll ask the same set of questions again. After reading what we have to say about successful retirement, hopefully you'll have a better handle on whether you're ready.

Summary

This chapter considers the research on attitudes toward retirement in workers approaching retirement age as opposed to attitudes of retirees toward retirement. For the most part, the research indicates that across almost every indicator, retirees are much more satisfied with retirement than they were before they actually retired. The one exception is satisfaction with finances in which increasing bankruptcies, a decline in housing prices, and a reduction in investment income have made the financial end of retirement more difficult for many retirees.

Useful Web Sites

Butrica, Barbara A., and Simone G. Schaner. July 2005. "Satisfaction and engagement in retirement." *Perspectives on Productive Aging*, no. 2. http://www. urban.org/UploadedPDF/311202_Perspectives2.pdf.

Fouquereau, E., A. Fernandez, and E. Mullet. 2001. "Evaluation of determinants of retirement satisfaction among workers and retired persons." http://findarticles.com/p/articles/mi_qa3852/is_200101/ai_n8928862.

Markham's Behavioral Health. 2006. "Retirement satisfaction not just about income." http://behavioralhealth.typepad.com/markhams_behavioral_healt/2006/04/retirement_sati.html.

Updegrave, Walter. January 13, 2006. "3 rules for a happy retirement." CNN.Money. http://money.cnn.com/2006/01/13/retirement/updegrave_money_0602/index.htm.

▓ References

Bakalar, N. "Retirement contentment in reach for unhappy men." *The New York Times*, April 4, 2006, http://www.nytimes.com/2006/04/04/health/psychology/04reti.html.

Brougham, R.R., and D. A. Walsh. 2005. "Goal expectations as predictors of retirement intentions." *International Journal of Aging and Human Development* 61(2): 141–60.

Danner, D. D., D. A. Snowdon, and W. V. Friesen. 2001. "Positive emotions in early life and longevity: Findings from the nun study." *Journal of Personality and Social Psychology* 80(5): 804–13.

Drentea, P. May, 2002. "Retirement and mental health." *Journal of Aging and Health* 14(2): 167–94.

Dugas, C. 2008. "Bankruptcy seniors." *USA Today*, June 21, 2008, http://www.usatoday.com/money/perfi/retirement/2008-06-16-bankruptcy-seniors_N.htm?POE=click-refer.

Gellene, D. 2007. "Loneliness often precedes elder dementia, study finds." *Los Angeles Times*, February 10, 2007, p. A11.

Health and Retirement Study. 2003. The HRS (2003) is a longitudinal survey of older Americans conducted by the Survey Research Center at the University of Michigan for the National Institute on Aging. For more information, see http://hrsonline.isr.umich.edu.

Jeste, D. 2005. "Successful Aging is Simply 'Mind over Matter.'" American College of Neuropsychopharmacology (ACNP) Annual Report.

MetLife Retirement Crossroads Study: Paving the Way to a Secure Future. February 2002. Rand Corporation.

Prince, M. J., R. H. Harwood, R. A. Blizard, and A. Thomas. 1997. "Social support deficits, loneliness and life events as risk factors for depression in old age: The Gospel Oak Project VI." *Psychological Medicine* 27:323–32.

Smith, D. B., and P. Moen. 2004. "Retirement satisfaction for retirees and their spouses: Do gender and the retirement decision-making process matter?" *Journal of Family Issues* 25:262.

Sorkin, D., K. S. Rook, and J. L. Lu. 2002. "Loneliness, lack of emotional support, lack of companionship, and the likelihood of having a heart condition in an elderly sample." *Annals of Behavioral Medicine* 24(4): 290–98.

Stern, L. 2008, "Recession and retirement." *Newsweek,* April 28, 151(17): 60–63.

Stossel, S. 2000. Lonely in America. [Interview with Robert Putnam.] *Atlantic Unbound,* September 21. www.theatlantic.com/unbound/interviews,ba2000-09-21.htm (accessed on June 16, 2008).

Vaillant, G. E., A. C. DiRago, and K. Mukamal. 2006. "Natural history of male psychological health VX: Retirement satisfaction." *American Journal of Psychiatry* 163:682–88. http://ajp.psychiatryonline.org/cgi/reprint/163/4/682?ck=nck.

Valliant, G. E., and Mukamal, K. 2001. "Successful aging." *American Journal of Psychiatry* 158(b): 839–847.

2 ▪ ▪ ▪

The Retirement Plan

Thinking about retirement as early in life as possible could certainly help you save sufficient amounts of money to retire and perhaps to do it early if this is your desire, but will it change your life once you've actually retired? Rosenkoetter and Garris (2001) asked just that question of more than 600 retired people and found that those who planned the most were the ones most involved in life after they retired. Those who reported no planning for retirement were inadequately prepared and reported that retirement was not what they thought it would be. The researchers also found that when retirement planning was done jointly with a spouse or mate, the adjustment to retirement was much better.

We doubt that people begin to think about the social and psychological aspects of retirement early in life. Why should they? Retirement may seem a long way off. However, they do think about the financial aspects of retirement early because pension and 401(k) decisions are often stressed by employers early in a worker's career. When do people begin to think seriously about retirement? We believe it begins to happen emotionally when we first begin to experience the signs of dissatisfaction and burnout with jobs and even with careers. Although this may not lead to a specific retirement plan, it does put the option on the table, and many workers begin a sort of pre-retirement dialogue with themselves years before they are actually ready to retire. In this chapter we'd like to consider the issues that one might think about in such a pre-retirement dialogue and how you might test some of your thoughts in the real world.

▨ Issues to Think About Well Before You're Ready to Retire

What does retirement represent?

For many of us, retirement represents the reward at the end of a long and productive life. It may be seen as an opportunity to rest and relax after many years of decidedly difficult work. For others, it may mean the ability to start new ventures and to do many of the things we always wanted to do but for which we had neither the time nor the income. And for some of us, retirement is a time to grow old with nothing to look forward to.

In a study of goals of retirement by age, Hershey and colleagues (2002) interviewed workers ranging in age from 20 to 67 and found that regardless of age, subjects felt strongly that retirement would increase their contact with others, increase leisure time, and lead to growth and creativity. So the first step in this exercise is for you to decide rationally what you think retirement will lead to and to test it out by understanding that if you have difficulty making friends now, how will retirement magically improve that situation? The answer is, of course, that it won't. How do we know?

Vaillant and Mukamal (2001) found that your lifestyle at age 50 is a solid predictor of what it will be when you retire. If you have healthy behaviors at 50, it's likely that those behaviors will continue after you retire. If you have an unhappy marriage, are prone to depression or unhappiness, have few friends, and worry a lot, chances are that, without help to change these behaviors, they will continue on after you retire. Retirement is not a magic cure for long-held problems; the first thing you should do is to compare your expectations for retirement with the reality of your present life. If there are areas of unhappiness or unhealthy living, it's easier to make changes before you retire, and as early as possible, than to wait until after you've retired.

An Example

John Amis, 61, is a divorced single male with a very good portfolio of investments. He is moderately happy with his job, but cannot say truthfully that he likes it or that he wants to stay with it. In early retirement he sees himself as having more time to do things he cannot do now because of the demands of his work and the level of fatigue he feels during the weekend. He has few friends, few special interests, doesn't think he wants to take on a second career, and admits that he bores easily. He feels neither happy nor unhappy at present. He's thought about retirement as something he could easily move into since he has no ties to his current job or community.

Amis told us, "It's difficult for me to see myself staying in a job when I can make as much in retirement. I'd like to live someplace serene and beautiful but I haven't thought about it much. I think about getting out of the boring life I have and hope that change will make my life better. On the checklist, I had a score of 95. I gave myself 5's mostly, but 8's and 9's on things like finances and health. I don't think my life will be much different after I retire except for not having to work at a job I don't like. Other things, such as meeting people and keeping busy, will take care of themselves, I think. I am who I am and retirement isn't going to change that."

We cautioned him against taking early retirement because his lack of planning and thoughtful reflection made him a bad candidate for early retirement. We suggested pre-retirement workshops and planning, but he retired nonetheless. A year later, he was back at another full-time job he didn't particularly like. He told us, "It beats sitting home all day watching soaps, that's for sure." Had he learned anything about retirement from the experience? "Yes," he told us. "I don't have enough life skills to be retired. Work is pretty much how I spend my time. The year I spent not working was agony. I'm seeing a retirement specialist to help me plan better for those things I know I'm no good at. The retirement specialist is helping me connect with people by joining groups in town and having a better social life. It's not counseling so much as it is advice and practical help connecting with other people and social activities. He thinks when I'm ready for retirement that I should consider a retirement community because there are many activities and lots of ways to connect with people. I've checked them out and they depress the hell out of me, but then maybe I'm not ready to think seriously about retirement. I was good at saving enough money for retirement but not very good about the other stuff that goes along with it. I feel like I'm getting a handle on myself but whether it will do any good when I'm retired, I'm not sure. I still feel bored and lonely on weekends and vacations make me miserable. I guess I have a while before I'll be ready for retirement." We agree, but at least he's working on it.

How do you handle free time?

Many of us believe incorrectly that we'll handle free time well in retirement, but the way you handle free time now is a predictor of how you'll handle free time in the future. The best way to check this out is to see how long it takes for you to feel bored on vacations. Many of you take work with you to prevent boredom, and some of you cut vacations short to return to work even when it isn't necessary. Be honest with yourself about how well you handle free time. If it's a tough question because you can't get a sense of your reaction from short vacation breaks, you may want to test the waters by taking advantage of a sabbatical and other paid leave programs available through your employment. Many companies have such programs, but often you'll need to look into them since they sometimes aren't widely advertised. Most involve developing a plan of activities that will benefit the organization, and some may involve living elsewhere.

Universities offer sabbaticals, which permit faculty members to take up to two semesters off for renewal and more in-depth research on subjects associated with your academic field. Often the first semester is at full pay, while two semesters off might reduce pay for the period to 50 percent. You are required to continue working for the organization a year or two for the length of the sabbatical or pay the sabbatical back, including benefits. Not only is this an excellent way to renew yourself and to do work you've wanted to do but were too busy to complete, but it's also a great way to test the waters for your ability to handle free time.

Organizations sometimes offer a phased retirement in which you have as long as five years to reduce the number of hours you work, with the difference made up through use of your pension. For example, the California State University system allows faculty members to retire, receive their full pension, and teach up to a 50 percent load for five years. Many faculty members use this as a way to transition to full retirement, but it also has financial benefits since pensions may not fully cover expenses. While the faculty member works, Social Security benefits increase, so when the phased retirement program ends, Social Security benefits have grown to an extent that they equate what the faculty member made were he or she still working full time.

An Example

One example of someone who used a sabbatical to test the retirement waters is Larry Anderson, a 59-year-old middle manager for a Kansas City software firm who liked his job but was worn out and needed a break. There was no sabbatical policy to provide him the needed time to renew himself from an extraordinary run of very demanding work assignments. Larry and his wife wanted to travel and take time off from a work life that was quickly affecting his health because of the high level of stress. His option was to resign, take his savings, and rest until he needed to find another job. In a long conversation with his wife, an alternative plan was developed, which he would share with his boss.

The plan was to propose a differential-in-pay leave. Larry would find a replacement for his job who would work at a salary somewhat lower than

Larry's. In some organizations, that amount would be up to half of the normal salary. Larry would advertise the position as a way to gain new experience for the short term. As an added incentive, he would offer to rent his house to the new person for a nominal fee. The house would be empty anyway, and finding a short-term renter made little sense.

As an incentive to the company, Larry promised to do marketing research in his travels and to return with a comprehensive report at the end of his leave. The company agreed that Larry needed a break, and agreed to the pay the differential salary to the new person as long as Larry found a person suitable for the job. Because Larry was well connected, he was soon able to find an out-of-work colleague with excellent qualifications to work in Larry's place for the year of his leave. The agreement was that Larry would receive half salary and full benefits during the year and that he would then return to his position full time. Larry's replacement would receive the other half of Larry's salary, a considerable improvement over unemployment compensation. If the replacement worked out, there would be an attempt to find him full-time work in the company, or in an allied company.

Larry spent a blissful time traveling for a year. He found himself renewed and ready to return to work with a full head of steam. His report saved the company much more than it may have lost in the arrangement, and his replacement now has a job with the company. These creative arrangements are possible in even the worst of business climates if you are willing to think through arrangements that benefit all parties involved.

This is not to say that phased retirement through sabbaticals and early retirement programs completely eliminate the need to prepare people to handle free time or make retirees more satisfied after full retirement. Reitzes and Mutran (2004) followed people in a phased retirement program for two years before retirement and two years after they retired. What they found was confirmation of Atchley's (1975, 1982) five stages of adjustment to retirement: (a) The *honeymoon period*, which is characterized as a euphoric period in which retirees relish their new freedom of time and space; (b) the *disenchantment period*, which reflects the emotional letdown as people face the reality of everyday life in retirement; (c) the *reorientation period*, which refers to the development of a realistic view of the social and economic opportunities and constraints of retirement; (d) the *stability period*, which occurs when people have achieved a certain accommodation and adjustment to retirement; and (e) the *termination period*, which denotes the eventual loss of independence due to illness and disability.

Reitzes and Mutran (2004) also found that (a) pre-retirement self-esteem and a rich social network, as well as pension eligibility, increased positive attitudes toward retirement throughout the 24-month period following retirement; and (b) retirement planning and voluntary retirement increased positive attitudes toward retirement in the initial period of retirement, but not later in the first two years of retirement. After the honeymoon period wore off, retirees had to deal with the realities of retirement that weren't completely understood during their phased-in pre-retirement period.

We think the reason people go through Atchley's phases are that retirement without work is a shock. We often think of work in its least satisfying way as a chore, something to do to keep us in food and shelter, but work gives us meaning—it offers status, it helps us fill our time, and it provides, at its best, intense satisfaction and friendships. This is why our next area of planning is to think about some form of continued work after retirement, but work that is satisfying and even new and innovative.

Should you continue to work after you retire?

According to Zedlewski and Butrica (2007), research evidence increasingly shows that older adults who regularly work after retirement enjoy better health and live longer, thanks to stimulating environments and a sense of purpose. Calvo (2006) found that paid work for older adults improves health. Tsai and colleagues (2005) followed a sample of early retirees for 30 years and found that they died earlier than workers who retired later. Dhaval and colleagues (2006) found that complete retirement without work decreases physical and mental health.

The reasons why work improves health is that it increases cognitive activity, exposure to stimulating environments, and social interactions (Kubzansky, Berkman, and Seeman 2000), enhances social status (Thoits and Hewitt, 2001), and offers greater access to social, psychological, and material resources (Wilson 2000). Some work-related activities help older adults develop knowledge and skills that boost their self-images and mental outlooks (Harlow-Rosentraub, Wilson, and Steele 2006).

Once older adults reach age 65, most will opt for retirement (Ekerdt, 1998). Although some individuals move from full-time work to full-time leisure, a substantial number remain in the labor force after they leave their career jobs (Hansson, DeKoekkoek, Neece, and Patterson, 1997). Many of these working "retired" adults are in "bridge-type jobs," which help them transition from long-term career positions to total retirement (Feldman, 1994; Mutchler, Burr, Pienta, and Massagli, 1997). Bridge jobs may be part-time work, self-employment, or temporary work, and often involve a combination of fewer hours, less stress or responsibility, greater flexibility, and fewer physical demands (Feldman, 1994). Bridge jobs offer possible remedies to older adults who are concerned about their financial security and to employers who face a labor shortage.

Because of downsizing, employers have been offering incentives to induce or force costly older workers into early retirement such that many older adults have left the labor force before reaching retirement age ("Business: The Jobs Challenge," 2001). By the late 1990s, early retirements accounted for more than 80 percent of total retirements (Seymour, 1999). A significant number of these early retirees participate in some form of bridge employment (Feldman, 1994).

Ulrich and Brott (2005) studied the strategies made by retirees to transition into bridging jobs. The following themes emerged: (a) The majority of the participants planned for their financial future but did not consider what they wanted to do after they retired. They did not take advantage of their community's career and job search resources. (b) Some individuals did not have to start over again because they were able to build on their past career experience, marketable skills, reputations, and personal skills. (c) Participants discovered that a bridge job sometimes introduced unwanted changes, such as lower pay, lack of career advancement, difficulties in forming close work relationships, separation from former career field, and loss of responsibilities. (d) Without sufficient planning or reaching out to available resources, many participants found it difficult to switch to a new career. They had a hard time moving into a new job if the job title did not match their long-term career title or if they defined their occupational field too narrowly. (e) Many did not fully investigate a job opportunity before they accepted employment and were disappointed after a period of time on the job. (f) Participants were reluctant to move into new jobs because they lacked the appropriate technological skills or they questioned their ability to learn these new skills. (g) Taking employment-related tests was viewed as an unpleasant experience for these older adults. (h) At the end of their long-term career or during their transition to a bridge job, many participants speculated that their careers and their transition efforts were affected by subtle age discrimination, such as younger employees questioning their capabilities. (i) Regardless of these challenges, participants benefited greatly from their bridge jobs. They credited their bridge jobs for making them feel better about themselves, giving them a more balanced life, and helping them *enjoy their work*. They felt better about themselves because what they continued to learn made a difference to others, demonstrated their competency, and made them feel healthy.

An Example

Betty Nelson, a Florida social worker, thought that she was about as burned out as she could be from a demanding job in child protective services. She and her husband (a physician in private practice) thought about retirement as a way to reduce the stress in their lives through travel and personal growth, but a year of complete retirement from work suggested that she was not ready to stop working. When her employer asked to her return to work part-time, she jumped at the chance and is now very happy working two days a week.

We asked her why she thought retirement would be so much better than work. "This may sound strange coming from someone who works with people and knows a lot about human behavior, but we were so caught up in our careers and the stress from our jobs that we never really thought about retirement as anything but a respite from stress. We thought we'd be older than we actually are. I mean that we thought we'd feel old when in fact we feel young. We thought we'd have health problems at age 65 but thank God we both are very healthy. We thought travel would be glamorous and exciting and it was—for maybe a month—and then it just became boring. We should have taken long trips or worked part-time or something to test out how we dealt with free time, but we didn't.

"The reality is that neither one of us likes a lot of free time and going back to work part time has been wonderful. I work the first two-and-a-half days of the week and John works the second two-and-half days of the week so we have what feels like a normal work week. We were getting into each other's hair and it was annoying. Now we feel grateful to have each other evenings and weekends, and we plan trips and have our dreams, but they're a lot more realistic. I would say that a reality check should be done throughout your adult life to check out your thinking about retirement. Be honest because we weren't and it led to a very troubled and unhappy year for us until we went back to work."

So yes, the evidence seems to suggest that some form of work is preferable to no work once you retire, but that should include a very wide range of definitions of work: part-time, consulting, self-employment, new careers, reduced hours on a current job, and other creative options.

Is work so bad that you need to quit and consider retirement as an option?

Older workers often have little choice in whether they continue working full-time. As Mor-Barak and Tynan (1993) point out, "Despite this interest in continued employment by employers and older adults, older workers are more likely to lose their jobs than younger workers in instances such as plant closings and corporate mergers (Beckett, 1988)" (p. 45). The authors go on to say that many businesses can't or won't deal with life events faced by older workers such as "widowhood and caring for ailing spouses, and as a result many older workers are forced to retire earlier than planned" (p. 45).

Writing about the loss of work and its impact on older men, Levant (1997) says that as men lose their good-provider roles, the experience results in "severe gender role strain" (p. 221) that affects relationships and can be disruptive to the point of ending otherwise strong marriages. Because older adults are more likely to lose high-level jobs because of downsizing and age discrimination, social contacts decrease and many otherwise healthy and motivated workers must deal with increased levels of isolation and loneliness. Schneider (1998) points out that many of us are workaholics and that when work is taken away or jobs are diminished in complexity and creativity, many older adults experience a decrease in physical and mental health. And while early retirement is touted as a way to achieve the good life at an early age, the experience is a complex and even wrenching one, in which older adults who are financially able to retire often have little ability to handle extra time, have failed to make sound retirement plans, and find out quickly that not working takes away social contacts, status, and a way to organize time.

For many healthy, work-oriented, and motivated older adults, volunteer and civic roles are not at all what they are looking for. They want to continue to work, to contribute, and to receive the financial and social status and benefits related to work. A looming labor shortage suggests that the American workplace will see many older workers continue to work at high-level, higher-paying jobs well into their 70s and beyond. The fact that Social Security has a benefit scale based on birth date will make it unlikely for many workers currently in their forties and fifties to retire early. This, of course, also has negative ramifications for workers who have worked at physically and emotionally demanding jobs and have seen their bodies wear out.

In an analysis of the impact of paid work and formal volunteerism, Zedlewski and Butrica (2007) found that numerous studies supported the finding that work and formal volunteering improved health, reduced the risk of serious illness and emotional difficulties such as depression, and improved strength and cognitive functioning, while full retirement without work and early loss of jobs increased the probability of illness and emotional difficulties. Clearly, having something of value to do after retirement is a protective factor in keeping older adults healthy and emotionally engaged with the world around them.

An Example

Jake Larson is someone who likes his job and has no plans to retire early. "I'm 68," he told us, "and I still feel a high when I go to work. I'm well taken care of financially and my wife keeps telling me we could see the world instead of my continuing to work, but to be truthful, I don't really want to see the world and she knows it. I like the folks I work with and the work is fun. I get razzed a lot about being too old to do the job but everyone knows how good I am at it. I see a lot of my friends who retired early and stopped working full time before they were ready and they're miserable. They didn't like their jobs and I told them that maybe doing something else would make the difference, but now they work at part-time jobs that pay next to nothing. One of them greets people at Wal-Mart. He's a smart guy who was a very successful appraiser but unhappy and now he greets people. I know that he hates it. He quit his job because he was burned out and wishes he was back at it but with the current housing market in a shambles he can't find anything else. I think planning for work after you retire is a necessity and if you like your job and you can keep working, I'd recommend that people do it. When I actually do retire, we'll be very comfortable financially. Just working these few years past 65 has made a real difference in our savings."

Will you be financially secure in retirement?

We will write extensively about this important subject in the next several chapters, but from personal experience what you save and invest early on and the performance of your investments at the beginning of your working career is a very important issue, which many younger workers are ill prepared to consider. They may understand the need to save, but know very little about investing, and too often rely on the people who come to their organizations to sell them retirement instruments. These folks are sales people for the most part. Don't rely on them. Look for a professional money manager or a fund manager with whom you can talk, find out about investing, and learn from them how best to protect your savings. They may charge for managing your investments (1 percent of the total investments they manage is a norm), but they're worth every penny, particularly in a down market. This doesn't mean that you can't learn about investing (you should), but until that time you need to think of an investment professional much as you think of doctors or lawyers as professionals you use when needed. In the next section on finances, we'll explain the best way to protect and grow your money during troubled economic times, and then we'll return to more on the social and emotional aspects of retirement.

■ Summary

In this chapter we discuss issues related to planning for retirement and suggest that you begin planning early enough to test the waters by considering whether you want to work longer, whether your work still gives you pleasure, how you handle free time, and whether you will be financially secure. We think this is a process that takes time and evolves. Trying to answer these questions a short time before you retire is unwise since this process may take several years or more and involves examining behaviors and situations that will be new to you.

■ Useful Web Sites

Motley Fool. How to Retire in Style (a number of issues covered in a series of links related to retirement planning). http://www.fool.com/Retirement/RetirementPlanning/RetirementPlanning01.htm

Planning Your Retirement: A number of useful links for *U.S. News and World Report.* http://www.usnews.com/Topics/tag/Series/p/planning_your_retirement/index.html

Planning for retirement: Top 10 things to know. CNNMONEY.COM http://money.cnn.com/magazines/moneymag/money101/lesson13/

Planning for Retirement: Your "to do" planner for a smooth transition (an excellent discussion of when to do various pre-retirement activities and what they entail). http://www.todaysseniors.com/pages/planning_for_retirement.html

U.S. Department of Labor. Taking the Mystery out of Retirement (an excellent guide to retirement planning with a number of chapters of relevance). http://www.dol.gov/ebsa/publications/nearretirement.html

■ References

Atchley, R. C. 1975. "Adjustment to the loss of job at retirement." *International Journal of Aging and Human Development* 6:17–27.

Atchley, R. C. 1982. "Retirement: Learning the world of work." *Annals of the American Academy of Political and Social Sciences* 464:120–31.

Beckett, J. O. 1988. "Plant closing: How older workers are affected." *Social Work* 33:29–33.

"Business: The jobs challenge." July 14, 2001. *The Economist* 360:56–57.

Calvo, E. 2006. "Does working longer make people healthier and happier?" *Work Opportunities for Older Americans,* Series 2. Chestnut Hill, MA: Center for Retirement Research, Boston College.

Dhaval, D., I. Rashad, I., and J. Spasojevic. 2006. "The effects of retirement on physical and mental health outcomes." NBER Working Paper 12123. Cambridge, MA: NBER.

Ekerdt, D. Workplace norms for the timing of retirement. In *Impact of work on older adults,* eds. K. Schaie and C. Schooler, 101–23. New York: Springer, 1998.

Feldman, D. C. 1994. "The decision to retire early: A review and conceptualization." *The Academy of Management Review* 19:285–311.

Hansson, R. O., P. D. DeKoekkoek, W. M. Neece, and D. W. Patterson. 1997. "Successful aging at work: Annual review, 1992–1996: The older worker and transition to retirement." *Journal of Vocational Behavior* 51:202–33.

Harlow-Rosentraub, K., L. Wilson, and J. Steele. "Expanding youth service concepts for older adults: Americorps results." In *Civic Engagement and the Baby Boomer Generation: Research, Policy and Practice Perspectives,* eds. L. Wilson and S. Simson, 61–84. New York: Haworth Press, 2006.

Hershey, D. A., J. M. Jacobs-Lawson, and K. A. Neukam. 2002. "Influences of age and gender on workers' goals for retirement." *International Journal of Aging and Human Development* 55(2): 163–79.

Kubzansky, L. D., L. F. Berkman, and T. E. Seeman. 2000. "Social conditions and distress in elderly persons: Findings from the MacArthur Studies of Successful Aging." *Journals of Gerontology: Psychological Science* 55b(4): 238–46.

Levant, R. F. 1997. "The masculinity issue." *Journal of Men's Studies* 5(3): 221–29.

Mor-Barak, M. E. and M. Tynan. January 1993. "Older workers and the workplace: A new challenge for occupational social work." *Social Work* 38(1): 45–55.

Mutchler, J. E., J. A. Burr, A. M. Pienta, and M. P. Massagli. 1997. "Pathways to labor force exit: Work transitions and work instability." *Journal of Gerontology: Social Sciences* 52b:S4–S12.

Reitzes, D. C., and E. J. Mutran. 2004. "The transition to retirement: Stages and factors that influence retirement adjustment." *International Journal of Aging and Human Development* 59(1): 63–84

Rosenkoetter, M. M., and J. M. Garris. 2001. *Issues in Mental Health Nursing* 22:703–22.

Schneider, K. J. 1998. "Toward a science of the heart: Romanticism and the revival of psychology." *American Psychologist* 53(3): 277–89.

Seymour, L. 1999. "Robust economy sends early retirements soaring to 81% of 1998 retirements." *Employee Benefit Plan Review* 54:50–51.

Thoits, P. A., and L. N. Hewitt. 2001. "Volunteer work and well-being." *Journal of Health and Social Behavior* 42(2): 115–31.

Tsai, S. P., J. K. Wendt, R. P. Donnelly, G. de Jong, and F. S. Ahmed. 2005. "Age at retirement and long-term survival of an industrial population: Prospective cohort study." *British Medical Journal* 331:995.

Ulrich, L. B., and P. E. Brott. December 2005. "Older workers and bridge employment: Redefining retirement." *Journal of Employment Counseling* 42: 159–70.

Vaillant, G. E., and K. Mukamal. 2001. "Successful aging." *American Journal of Psychiatry* 158(6): 839–47.

Wilson, J. 2000. "Volunteering." *Annual Review of Sociology* 26:215–40.

Zedlewski, S. R., and B. A. Burtrica. December 2007. "Are we taking full advantage of older adults' potential?" *The Retirement Project: Perspectives of Productive Aging*. The Urban Institute, 9.

Part II

THE FINANCIAL CRIB SHEET

This part of the book is intended to give you an introduction to the process of planning your retirement finances. It will explain:

1. How to develop a spending plan.
2. How to identify the major costs and risks of retirement financing.
3. How to utilize a simple equation to determine the amount of retirement income you have and need.
4. Two basic ways to fund your retirement with your savings.
5. Ideas to stretch your retirement income and savings.
6. Investment options and things to watch out for.
7. How to find a financial professional.
8. Basic insurance and estate planning needs.

This part of the book is not intended to tell you how to "double your money and retire a gazillionaire." The place for that is late-night infomercials. This book is also not intended to substitute for developing your own rigorous financial plan, or to tell you exactly what you should invest your retirement savings in or why.

Instead, this section will help individuals who are in or approaching retirement to determine how much they need to live on (the spending plan) and what amount of income they can develop from their retirement savings. For those who are several years from retirement, this section will help you determine what level of savings and investment is needed to fund your desired retirement lifestyle.

Approaching retirement from the standpoint of "I'm turning 65—and I'm going to retire no matter what" can be very dangerous and often very disappointing. It is important to recognize the consequences of retiring with limited savings or spending habits that outpace your income. This book is intended to help you understand just that.

3 ▪ ▪ ▪

The Retirement Equation

Financial planning, in its simplest form, is all about *cash flow management*: how we manage our paychecks while working, how we do or don't save for the future, how we protect ourselves financially, and how we manage our assets and spending throughout retirement. Topics within financial planning include, but are not limited to: saving for retirement, budgeting, tax strategies, retirement timing and income planning, insurance needs and planning, estate planning, and legacy planning.

Financial planning, put another way, is for most of us all about finding *balance*. Most of us need to find a way to live within our means, save for retirement (and college, and a new house, and ..., and maintain that balance throughout retirement. In 2008, the global economy and stock markets experienced one of the most significant contractions in a generation. For many caught unaware, retirement funds and long-term plans were drastically altered in a matter of weeks.

This book is for those who are beginning to think about retirement, for those who have recently retired, and even for those who are many years away from retirement. However, those who may benefit most at this point are part of the baby boomer generation, the oldest of whom are turning 62 in 2008. According to a 2004 Federal Reserve Board study, the median net worth of those aged 55–64 was $248,700, whereas the mean (average) was $843,800, indicating that the mean is skewed by fewer with much higher net worth (Federal Reserve Bank, 2006). This data indicates that half of all those surveyed, ages 55 to 64, have a net worth of less than $248,700. With 50 percent of all baby boomers having less than $248,700 in net worth, they will, without proper planning, likely find their retirement dreams severely curtailed unless they understand the limitations of their assets and retirement savings and have a clear idea of what those assets need to support over a 20- to 30-year retirement period. According to a 2008 retirement confidence survey (RCS) performed by the Employee Benefit Research Institute (EBRI), the confidence of current and future retirees has dropped significantly recently; only 18 percent of workers and 29 percent of retirees were feeling very confident about having enough money for retirement. This isn't too surprising considering that the study also found that only 72 percent of workers have saved anything for retirement and 49 percent of workers have saved less than $50,000. The level of retirement planning has increased slightly, but 43 percent of workers still guess how much they'll actually need for retirement.

These are truly alarming findings by the EBRI. Given the economic climate conditions that began in 2008, now, more than ever, pre- and current retirees need to get a clear grasp of their personal financial situation. This book will help you do just that.

Many things are outside of our control when it comes to financial planning. We don't know how long we'll live; we don't know how healthy we'll be in retirement; we don't know when the stock market will go up or down. However, there are many things that are within our control: we can (usually) decide when to retire; we can determine how much we need to live on; we can choose how much we want to or can spend on discretionary items; we can determine how much we should be saving; and we can decide whether or not we want to live within our means.

Financial planning is about finding balance. Preparing and saving for retirement requires meeting current income needs with saving for the future; retirees balance their current spending against existing assets to ensure that they don't outlive their money, but also to allow enjoyment of the retirement they have worked so long for.

Financial planning is a constant *process* of finding and maintaining balance. Honest communication with yourself, your spouse, and any professionals you use for help are critical to planning a successful retirement—at least financially.

What is a financially successful retirement? That answer is different for everyone, but for this text, we'll define a financially successful retirement as meeting financial obligations necessary to ensure that you keep a roof over your head, keep all the utilities turned on, and have the resources necessary to maintain your health without a great risk of outliving your assets.

The two critical components to understand are not only what you need to keep the lights on and the bills paid, but also what assets are needed to support those obligations over a potentially long retirement period. For some, it will be 30 years or more. This means two things: budgets and savings.

We are most concerned with determining what income is required to sustain required—or desired—living expenses over a potentially long period of retirement. We will also be determining what the sources of that income will be and the necessary retirement savings, and balancing the retirement income with the retirement expenses. This is best done with the Retirement Equation:

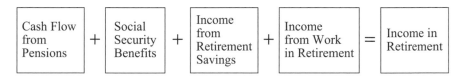

The Retirement Equation is meant to break down a simple concept to even simpler terms. As in any mathematical equation, values on both sides of the equal sign must be the same, or balance. Using the Retirement Equation, we can easily break down the equation into its individual components—add or subtract sources of income—and analyze each one.

■ Retirement Equation Components

Let's look at each of the Retirement Equation components:

> Cash Flow
> from
> Pensions

In 1980, 60 percent of workers who were in the private sector were covered by defined-benefit pensions. In 2006, only 8 percent of workers were covered, according to a paper from the Center for Retirement Research at Boston College (Boston College, 2008). If you're fortunate enough to retire with a full, or even partial, pension from a private corporation or government position, this will likely cover a large portion of your preretirement income. We'll discuss pensions more in a future chapter.

If you're near retirement age now in 2009, the likelihood of any changes to the Social Security system is remote. Retirement benefits from Social Security are based on your average earnings during a lifetime of work under the Social Security system. For most current and future retirees, the benefits will be based on the average of the 35 highest years of earnings. Years in which there are low earnings or no earnings may be counted to bring the total years of earnings up to 35.

Most workers have access to retirement plans through their employers, in the form of a 401(k) or something similar. Anyone who has earned income can also save for retirement with an Individual Retirement Account (IRA), either tax-deferred or after-tax. Assets for retirement don't necessarily have to be from retirement accounts, but can also be taxable investment accounts or assets from the sale of a business that are then invested.

> Income
> from
> Work in
> Retirement

Working after retirement may sound counterintuitive, but income from working in retirement may be the one thing that provides enough cash flow to make retirement possible. Work in retirement may include part-time employment from your previous employer, consulting work in your field of expertise, or somehow turning a hobby into a cash-generating business.

> Income
> in
> Retirement

Income in retirement can be either the starting point or the end point of the Retirement Equation. It can be the starting point by determining how much you spend now, or need to spend in order to maintain your desired lifestyle, and then determining the amount of savings you need. It can also be the end point of the Retirement Equation. If you are about to retire, or are already retired, and have saved all that you can for retirement, then those assets can provide only a certain amount without you running the risk of running out of assets early in retirement. That amount will be the Income in Retirement possible, or the result of the Retirement Equation.

In the following chapters, we'll consider all five parts of the Retirement Equation. We'll discuss the process of developing a spending plan, the major expected costs in retirement, ways to generate cash flow from retirement savings, and most importantly, using all of the data to balance the

Retirement Equation. We'll use multiple examples throughout the book, which will hopefully inspire you to then begin the process yourself and to eventually balance your own Retirement Equation.

▓ References

Bucks, Brian K., Arthur B. Kennickell, and Kevin B. Moore. 2006. "Recent Changes in U.S. Family Finances: Evidence from the 2001 and 2004 Survey of Consumer Finances." Federal Reserve Bulletin, March 2006.

Helman, Ruth, Mathew Greenwalk & Associates, Jack VanDerhei, and Craig Copeland. 2008. "The 2008 Retirement Confidence Survey: Americans Much More Worried About Retirement, Health Costs a Big Concern." Employee Benefit Research Institute. Issue Brief No. 316 April 2008.

Munnell, Alicia H., Jean-Pierre Aubry, and Dan Muldoon. 2008. The Financial Crisis and Private Defined Benefit Plans. Center for Retirement Research at Boston College, November 2008, Number 8–18.

4 ▪ ▪ ▪

Developing a Spending Plan

The word *budget* elicits strong emotional responses in people, usually negative. The idea of creating and adhering to a budget for some is impossible sometimes only because of what the word means to them. Perhaps the best approach is to avoid the use of the word. That's why, for the rest of the book, we'll refer to the process suggested by the B-word as a *spending plan*.

Almost half of all workers live paycheck to paycheck, according to a survey by CareerBuilder.com, including 21 percent of the people making $100,000 or more per year (Gurion, 2008). Spending is either discretionary or nondiscretionary, and you have control over both, especially the discretionary spending. As home prices across the country continue to fall, and credit continues to contract, the days of using a house as a personal ATM to purchase oversized SUVs and extra homes would appear to be over. Instead, there are numerous articles and blogs published about the virtues of frugality and a new idea for big purchases: the lay-away plan. Sometimes it takes a major financial crisis, like the one in 2008, to encourage us to review our spending habits and make us see what really is necessary and what is truly just a luxury.

■ Nondiscretionary Spending

Nondiscretionary spending is what we have to spend each month to keep a roof over our head and food on the table. We are less able to change this in the short term, but the choices we make can have a dramatic effect on the long-term costs associated with nondiscretionary expenses.

Housing is usually the largest nondiscretionary item in everyone's budget. As home prices rose rapidly, many people sold their houses and upgraded, and the average size of the American house rose from 1,600 square feet in the 1970s to more than 2,300 square feet today, according to the National Association of Home Builders (NAHB, 2008). With that added space comes increased costs from taxes, maintenance, and utilities, all while the average size of the American family is decreasing.

Another item that *should* be a nondiscretionary spending item is personal savings. Most of us have heard the phrase *pay yourself first* from many financial sources. This means with every paycheck, set some savings aside for retirement, emergencies, or the next big discretionary purchase. The personal savings rate has declined from about 10 percent in the early 1980s to about 2 percent of personal discretionary income during the last decade (FRBSF, 2005).

The choices we make regarding nondiscretionary spending can have long-term ramifications. Most of us would like a newer, larger house, or a new car every three years instead of every seven or eight or more. But for the majority of us, satisfying those wants now can have serious long-term impacts and can be the determinate force in whether we have a successful retirement, and in some cases, any retirement at all.

■ Discretionary Spending

What we spend, after we pay ourselves, and after we pay all the bills to keep the lights on, is discretionary spending. Trips to the coffee shop, entertainment, vacations, and extra movie channels are all discretionary expenses. After you've paid your bills, do you know where all your money goes?

Start writing down what you spend. Keep a small notepad in your pocket or purse. Each time you make a purchase, either in cash or as a charge to your credit card, write down the amount. At the end of the month, total the amounts recorded in the notepad, plus any bills paid directly from your bank account. You will be surprised by how much you are spending, and how little you have to show for it. By having the discipline to write down each purchase, you will likely find yourself beginning to question many purchases.

■ Making Decisions

What are your spending and saving goals? Do you have any? Are you meeting them? If you're not doing the things you'd like to do in retirement—perhaps you feel that you should be able to travel more or eat at nicer restaurants—then review your spending habits and create your spending plan to reallocate your priorities. It should only take one or two months of tracking your spending to determine whether or not your spending is aligned with your spending goals.

If you do have income left over after paying all your nondiscretionary bills, you do have choices regarding how remaining funds are spent according to your spending plan. It only takes a couple minutes to write down what you'd like to be able to do, whether it's save more for retirement or take at least one nice trip per year. What is that amount per month? Does it fit within your income after you've paid your bills? If the answer is yes, but you haven't been able to do what you'd like, now is the time to decide what you want to spend your money on and figure out a way to develop a balance between spending now, versus meeting, your spending goals.

■ Ideas to Help You Stick to the Plan

It was much easier to stick within a spending plan before the advent of debit cards and easy credit. Try using cash. If you use your debit card each time you buy groceries and also take cash out for miscellaneous spending, it's much more difficult to keep track of where that extra cash goes. It is also often the case that when using debit or credit, you're much more likely to spend more, as consumers simply feel the pain more when parting with cash (LifeScience, 2008). Some people find that cash is always burning a hole in their pocket, and if they don't have it, they won't spend it. However, one solution to both issues is to decide ahead of time how much you're going to spend on certain items, both discretionary and nondiscretionary.

When developing your spending plan, determine what you usually spend and what you *want* to spend considering your level of income. Does it make sense to spend $400 per month on specialty coffee drinks and lunches out if your income is only $25,000 per year? Most people would say no. What about groceries? What do you spend, and what do you think you could or should spend? A helpful solution is to decide ahead and pull that amount out in cash at the beginning of each month. If you feel that $400 is all that you really need and want to spend on groceries each month, put $400 in an envelope and don't spend more than that. If you decide that $400 is too much on coffee, and you decide that you can make do with only spending $250 per month on coffee and eating lunch out, pull that amount out of the bank and keep the cash in a separate place.

Savings as Part of a Spending Plan

Just because you're retiring, it doesn't mean that you need to stop saving. If your spending plan in retirement allocates $10,000 per year for travel, set up a separate savings account and automatically divert some of each income source to fund those plans.

If your retirement spending plan states that you'll spend $3,600 each year on home maintenance, it is unlikely that you'll spend exactly $300 per month. It's more likely you will spend in greater amounts when the house has to be repainted, the furnace finally quits, or the roof needs to be replaced. By maintaining a sound spending plan and continuing to save even in retirement, the large and unexpected expenses won't stop you from traveling, for example, for the next two or three years.

The same concept applies to any other large expense. Instead of expanding personal debt to take vacations, plan ahead and start putting aside funds each month until you reach your spending goal. It is very simple to set up an automatic transfer between bank accounts so paying yourself first is easy.

Working Together

Creating a spending plan is very simple for one. Add a spouse or partner with different ideas, and the process becomes much more difficult. In 2007, Fidelity Investments conducted research on the preparedness of pre-retiree baby boomers and their spouses to meet unexpected challenges in retirement. The research found that only 23 percent of couples partner in both day-to-day and long-term financial planning and are confident with themselves and each other's abilities to take full responsibility for financial decisions. These couples are more optimistic with regard to their expected lifestyles in retirement and are better prepared to meet unexpected challenges in retirement (Fidelity, 2007). On the other hand, couples that do not partner on financial decisions are less prepared.

Frugality

From the online encyclopedia Wikipedia we learn:
Frugality is the practice of:

1. acquiring goods and services in a restrained manner,
2. resourcefully using already owned economic goods and services, and
3. achieving a longer-term goal.

Note that this definition does not include the words *budgeting*, *cheap*, or *stingy*. Frugality is all about finding balance and allocating your available resources to achieve *more* of what you want to accomplish with your available resources. Frugality is about being creative and resourceful. If you have a retirement goal of at least one nice trip each year, you may find that the funds aren't available to stay in the nicest resorts and to eat every meal out—but the resources are there to rent a nice house or apartment and cook most of your meals in. This still allows you to reach your goals and, hopefully, still enjoy retirement.

■ References

Gurion, Hope. 2008. "Living Paycheck to Paycheck." CNN. http://www.cnn.com/2008/LIVING/worklife/10/08/cb.workers.paycheck/index.html

Federal Reserve Bank of San Francisco. 2005. "Ask Dr. Econ: Are 401k and IRA contributions included in the national savings rate and if so how is this calculated?" http://www.frbsf.org/education/activities/drecon/answerxml.cfm?selectedurl=/2005/0508.html.

Fidelity. 2007. 2007 Fidelity Married Couples Research. personal.fidelity.com/myfidelity/InsideFidelity/NewsCenter/mediadocs/couples_research_exec_summary.pdf.

LiveScience. 2008. "Study: Credit Cards Cause More Spending." http://www.livescience.com/culture/080907-cash-credit.html.

National Association of Home Builders. 2008. http://www.nahb.org/news_details.aspx?newsID=7429.

5 ▪ ▪ ▪

The Cost of Retirement

Personal finance books and Internet resources often approach the process of planning for retirement incorrectly. Many retirement information sources, for example, say that you need 80 percent of your salary each year when you retire. Other resources say you need 60 percent, or somewhere between 90 percent and 120 percent. While this may be a rough starting point, it only takes a little more effort to determine—with much more precision—what you really need in terms of income or assets to generate the required cash flow for retirement living expenses. Utilizing the Retirement Equation presented in the previous chapter, we're going to work through an example of balancing a budget with available assets to fund that retirement budget.

▪ The Three Major Costs in Retirement: Health Care, Inflation, and Housing

What does financial independence cost in retirement? Is it just a matter of covering a few utility bills and golf or tennis club dues? Where does health care fit into your grand retirement scheme? Do you think that Medicare will pick up all your medical bills once you reach 65? Do you still have a mortgage on your home? What will the effects of inflation do to your retirement nest egg over the course of 20 years or more? Do you know *exactly* how long you'll live? These are important questions you'll need to think through carefully as you consider how much money you will need to pay for retirement.

In this chapter we'll help you break down the major costs in retirement. There is significant research available on the expected costs of health care in retirement, in addition to Medicare. We'll also discuss the true costs of housing, the advantages and disadvantages of having a mortgage in retirement, and the long-term, deleterious effects of inflation on your purchasing power.

▓ Health Care Costs in Retirement

In recent years we've all enjoyed the tremendous growth in medical technology and research. There seems to be a magic pill for every ailment, and life expectancy continues to increase. The biggest issue with trying to determine how much we will need to save to cover our retirement expenses is that we just don't know how long we're going to live. According to an Employee Benefit Research Institute report in 2004, a 65-year-old man in good health has a life expectancy of 82. A 65-year-old woman in good health has a life expectancy of 86 (EBRI, 2004). Of course, some will live longer and some won't make it to the average life expectancy. In fact, 25 percent of the population over 65 will live well into their nineties. Medical research and technology continue to grant us longer and healthier lives. The probability that more of us will live to be 90 or 100 is increasing every year.

Another EBRI study in 2008 stated that couples who purchase Medigap and Medicare Part D prescription drug coverage at age 65 will need to save anywhere from $194,000 to $635,000 depending on their use of prescription drugs (EBRI, 2008). According to the study, a couple with median prescription drug needs will need $194,000 in savings to have a 50 percent chance of having enough saved to cover their prescription drug needs. If that same couple wants a 90 percent chance of having enough savings to cover their prescription drug costs, they will need to have saved $305,000. When a couple needs more prescription drug coverage than 90 percent of the population and wants a 90 percent chance of having saved enough to cover those costs, they will need $635,000.

According to this data, a man with expected prescription drug costs at the median (50 percent of retirees spent more on prescription drugs, 50 percent of retirees spent less) would need at least $79,000 if he had a goal of having a 50 percent chance of having enough money to cover

Table 5.1
Savings Needed for Medigap Premiums, Medicare Part B Premiums,
Medicare Part D Premiums, and Out-of-Pocket Drug Expenses for
Retirement at Age 65 in 2008

	Median Prescription Drug Expenses Throughout Retirement	75th Percentile of Prescription Drug Expenses Throughout Retirement	90th Percentile of Prescription Drug Expenses Throughout Retirement
Men			
Median	$79,000	$93,000	$156,000
75th Percentile	122,000	144,000	248,000
90th Percentile	159,000	189,000	331,000
Women			
Median	108,000	127,000	217,000
75th Percentile	143,000	170,000	296,000
90th Percentile	184,000	220,000	390,000
Married Couple			
Median	194,000	228,000	390,000
75th Percentile	253,000	299,000	518,000
90th Percentile	305,000	363,000	635,000

Source: EBRI Issue Brief No. 317, May 2008, Figure 2.

health care expenses in retirement. If that man had prescription drug
needs in the 90th percentile (he spends more on prescription drugs than
90 percent of all other retirees), and he also wants to be 90 percent sure
that he has enough saved to cover health care expenses in retirement, he
will need to have saved $331,000.

This study does not include costs associated with long-term care or
assisted living, which in 2007, averaged $77,745 for a private long-term
care room per year (AARP, 2007). We will talk much more about the various Medigap plans and the costs associated with deductibles and out-of-
pocket expenses in a later chapter on health care, but you can see that
health care costs are a major issue to consider in preparing your retirement budget.

▨ Inflation

The rapid increase in health care costs is a key example of why it is important to protect retirement assets from the destruction of purchasing power
due to inflation. What is inflation? There are many definitions and

numerous technical explanations, but the simple definition is: a rise in the general level of prices of goods and services over time.

The Bureau of Labor Statistics (BLS), a division of the U.S. Department of Labor, publishes monthly data for inflation in the United States called the Consumer Price Index, or CPI. The BLS publishes a number of different data points, but we're most interested in the CPI-U, which is a measure of inflation for urban wage earners and clerical workers, professional, managerial, and technical workers, the self-employed, short-term workers, the unemployed, retirees, and others not in the labor force (BLS, 2008).

Data for the CPI-U is available from the Bureau of Labor Statistics going back to 1913. The average inflation rate, as measured by the CPI-U since 1913 has been 3.43 percent per year, with a high annual rate of 20.4 percent in 1918 and a low annual change of -10.3 percent in 1921. For the last 20 years, the CPI-U data has averaged 3.17 percent in annual increases, but with fewer significant changes. The highest CPI-U annual change since 1988 was 6.1 percent in 1990, and the smallest change was 1.6 percent in both 1998 and 2001.

A typical assumption for retirement planning has been that inflation increases, on average, 3 percent per year. CPI-U data suggests that assumption is low, particularly if you consider that the Employee Benefit Research Institute found that the average annual inflation rise for Medicare beneficiaries was 7.2 percent during the 2003–2007 period (EBRI Issue Brief No. 317, May 2008). Further, in 2004, Medicare Part B premiums increased 17.4 percent, while premiums rose 13 percent in both 2003 and 2005.

It is readily apparent that health care inflation is much greater than the 3 percent figure most people use as an average inflation rate for retirement planning. An aggregate rate is much more likely to be 4 percent a year or higher. The greater the percentage of your retirement dollars that goes for health care, the more inflation eats away at your total savings.

A single year of 3 percent or 6 percent inflation isn't necessarily a huge impediment to retirement, but 10, 20, or 30 years of 4 percent inflation is. If a retiree begins retirement with $40,000 of annual expenses, with inflation at 4 percent per year, in 20 years they will require $87,645 to cover the same expenses.

Many savers and retirees like to utilize Certificates of Deposits (CDs) because they're safe (they are insured by the Federal Deposit Insurance Corporation) and they guarantee a known interest and return of principal at maturity. However, inflation can make what seems like a safe and generous investment a losing proposition. Consider the following example of using CDs as a source of retirement income.

An example

Marcia, 65, has always used CDs at her local bank for savings and to generate income to pay her bills. Each time a CD matures, Marcia puts the interest in her checking account to pay expenses and the principal back into a new 12-month CD. Marcia currently has $500,000 in deposits earning 4 percent, or $20,000 per year, which is enough to cover her expenses beyond her Social Security benefits. The problem is, Marcia is spending the entire $20,000, and not considering what inflation will do to her purchasing power over time. If we assume that inflation is 4 percent, in 10 years the $20,000 will only purchase about $13,500 worth of goods and services. Plus, Marcia will still only have $500,000 in the bank, which is more like $337,782 after 10 years of inflation. After 20 years of 4 percent inflation, the income and principal will have the purchasing power of $9,127 and $228,200, respectively.

The following graph clearly shows the effect of 4 percent inflation on purchasing power.

After 30 years of 2 percent inflation, $1.81 is required to maintain the purchasing power of every $1; at 3 percent inflation, $2.42; at 4 percent inflation, $3.24; and at 5 percent inflation, $4.32.

How can you protect yourself against the effects of inflation? The advantage of working is that every year or so, most employers give a cost-of-living adjustment to your wages to help offset the effect of inflation. But now, in retirement, you're required to create your own cost-of-living adjustment. We'll go much further into this in later chapters, but the simple explanation is that you must earn a return on your retirement assets that is greater than the rate of inflation.

Fortunately, each year the Social Security Administration makes cost-of-living adjustments, or COLAs, based on the rate of inflation in the prior year. Unfortunately, the COLA is inadequate to keep pace with dramatic

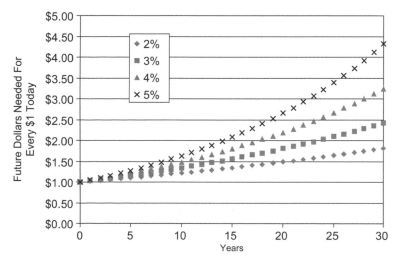

Figure 5.1
Inflation Effects on Purchasing Power

increases in the cost of living. The COLA in fall 2007 was only 2.3 percent while the inflation rate for 2007 was more than 4 percent—and much higher in the important areas of energy and food, which saw increases of 15 percent in the first half of the year. Those on Social Security must make up the difference through the growth of savings and investments.

■ Housing

According to a 2007 Housing and Urban Development study, the median housing expense for owner-occupied homes is 24 percent of total household income. A 2007 U.S. Census Bureau study found that 37.5 percent of mortgaged homeowners spent more than 30 percent of their household income on housing expenses (U.S. Census Bureau, 2007). This is quite high, and given the economic conditions we experienced in 2008, that number is likely to be higher now. According to a Federal Reserve Survey of Consumer Finances, 32 percent of households headed by someone age 65 to 74 were carrying home-mortgage debt as of 2001, up from 26 percent three years earlier (Clements, 2004).

We think it makes a good deal of sense to try and pay off a mortgage as soon as possible either before or after you retire. Not having a mortgage payment to worry about not only reduces the amount of money you spend each month, but over the total years of your retirement, it can make a large difference, as the following example suggests.

An example

A couple are about to retire at 65 and have just purchased a new home. They purchased the home with a 30-year fixed mortgage with a payment of $1,200 per month. If they wanted to invest enough money to cover the mortgage payment of $1,200 per month, and they were planning on using an annual withdrawal rate of 4 percent from their investments, they would need $360,000 invested to cover their mortgage (12 × $1,200 = $14,400 ÷ 4% = $360,000). If this couple could have entered retirement without a mortgage, and still had that $360,000 saved, they could use that $14,400 each year for other retirement goals.

Maintaining mortgage debt in retirement can strangle the retirement spending plan. Retirees are often faced with the tough choice of either cutting back on what they would rather be doing in retirement, such as traveling and entertaining, or working longer to pay the mortgage, or both. One argument for keeping a mortgage is the large tax deduction on the interest paid. It is important to remember that toward the end of the mortgage repayment period, the majority of the monthly payment is principal, not interest, which decreases the tax benefit. We feel that it makes most sense to use your last paycheck to make your last mortgage payment.

If you don't currently own your own home, but you rent, or have always rented, does it make sense to buy a home at retirement? There are certainly advantages to renting a home—for starters, the average rent is less than the cost of a home, even after the dramatic home price declines we saw in 2008.

The price-rent ratio is a common tool to measure when home prices have risen too far, or when rents are especially attractive compared to what an equivalent home could be purchased for. The price-rent ratio is the cost of a home divided by the annual rent of an equivalent home. In June 2007, the price-rent ratio was at an average of 22.8 for the nation. The 15-year average price-rent ratio is 16.9 (*Fortune*, 2007). For example, a monthly rent of $1,000 would be equivalent to owning a $202,800 house (12 × $1,000 × 16.9 = $202,800). As of June 2007, that same $1,000 rent payment would be similar to owning a $273,600 home (12 × $1,000 × 22.8 = $273,600). Clearly, renters have been getting the better deal, especially when considering the recent dramatic declines in home prices. The combination of lower equivalent rents, lower maintenance costs, property taxes wrapped into the monthly rent, and the ability to relocate more easily are all benefits of remaining a renter if that is your current situation.

▨ The Retirement Budget: The Right Side of the Retirement Equation

Here is a simple variation on the Retirement Equation presented in the previous chapter:

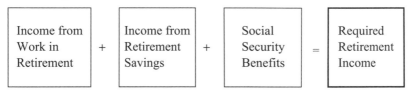

We know that the combined income from work in retirement, plus cash flow generated from retirement and investment accounts, plus Social Security benefits all add up to a total amount of annual income to fund annual expenses in retirement. We're going to start on the right side of the equation, as most of us do not have unlimited funds to finance any lifestyle we choose. We want to know what it is that we must pay for each month and also what we would like to do in retirement that requires additional income.

Now, it's time to get out your paper, pencil, and calculator and create a budget that accurately identifies what you actually must spend each month to pay your bills.

Below is the beginning of an example that we'll discuss throughout the next few chapters. A couple, Luke and Sarah, who are both 65 years old, are about to retire with the following assets:

Assets Available

1.	Luke: 401(k) retirement account:	$135,000
2.	Sarah: 401(k) retirement account:	$150,000
3.	Joint Investment Account:	$205,000
4.	Emergency Cash Fund:	$ 36,000
Total Savings:		**$526,000**

Last Year's Income:

1. Luke: $45,000
2. Sarah: $45,000

Below is a spending plan that Luke and Sarah have developed to estimate what they would like to spend in retirement. You should use this as an outline for your own retirement spending plan.

The budget totals are before taxes, that is, the totals are the amounts you actually see going out to pay expenses. When you withdraw funds from retirement accounts that were tax deferred, you will pay income tax on the amount withdrawn. Tax rates will vary widely between individuals and this is beyond the scope of this book. For the sake of simplicity, we're assuming an effective total tax rate of 10 percent. For example, if you need to spend $1,000 and that $1,000 comes from your retirement account, you'll need to withdraw more to cover the expected taxes. In this example, $1,000 of required income would have $100 in taxes, therefore, the total amount to withdraw would be $1,100, with $1,000 going to pay the required expense and $100 to pay taxes. Retirees will need to factor that into their annual budgets.

	Annual	Monthly
10% Income Tax	$5,964	$497
Total Required Retirement Income	$65,608	$ 5,467

Another important point to note about the above budget is that it does not include savings for retirement or investment accounts. This is typically a fact that is overlooked when pre-retirees begin the initial planning process that can free up a considerable amount of cash flow depending on how much was saved on a regular basis.

Income from Work in Retirement	+	Income from Retirement Savings	+	**Social Security Benefits**	=	Required Retirement Income

■ The Left Side of the Retirement Equation: Social Security

If you're near or at retirement age, there shouldn't be any question about collecting income from Social Security. If you want to know how much you'll receive or how to apply for benefits, just about every question you

Table 5.2
Spending Plan Example

Category	Description	Annual	Monthly
Housing	Property Taxes	$ 3,000	$ 250
	Insurance	$ 1,200	$ 100
	Heating, Electricity, etc.	$ 6,000	$ 500
	Phone	$ 1,440	$ 120
	Maintenance	$ 2,500	$ 208
	Home Supplies	$ 600	$ 50
	Miscellaneous	$ 500	$ 60
	Mortgage / Rent	$ 7,200	$ 600
Car	Insurance	$ 600	$ 50
	Gas	$ 1,200	$ 100
	License	$ 120	$ 10
	Maintenance	$ 360	$ 30
	Payment	$ 3,600	$ 300
Food	Groceries	$ 4,800	$ 400
Pets	Food	$ 240	$ 20
	License	$ 24	$ 2
	Veterinarian	$ 100	$ 8
Personal	Healthcare	$ 9,000	$ 750
	Clothing	$ 500	$ 42
	Miscellaneous	$ 1,200	$ 100
	Health Club	$ 960	$ 80
Luxuries	Travel	$ 8,000	$ 667
	Entertainment	$ 4,800	$ 400
	Gifts	$ 500	$ 42
	Personal	$ 1,200	$ 100
Total Before-Income Tax Required		$59,644	$ 4,970

can imagine can be found online at the Social Security Administration Web site, www.ssa.gov. One benefit of going to the Web site is utilizing the Social Security "Quick Calculator" to estimate your future benefits.

To continue with our Retirement Equation example, we'll assume that Luke and Sarah will retire at the same time, and at the same age—65 years old. Both earned $45,000 per year in their last year of employment. According to the SSA Quick Calculator, each retiree will collect approximately $1,113 per month in the year they retire, or $2,226 combined per month.

There is a lot of debate regarding the correct age to begin taking Social Security benefits. There probably isn't a perfect answer, but generally, you start taking benefits as soon as you retire. We're assuming, for the purposes of this book, that you retire at the age in which you will receive full benefits.

Your benefits depend on when you were born. People who were born in 1940 don't begin collecting full benefits until they're 65.5. The younger you are, the later your retirement date for full benefits. If you retire earlier (you can begin taking benefits at age 62 if you are Social Security eligible), your benefit will be about a fifth less than your full benefit. Remember that you cannot earn more than your yearly benefit without being taxed a dollar for every dollar over your yearly benefit if you begin taking benefits before your full benefit date. If you begin taking benefits after your full benefit date, you can earn as much as you'd like and not lose Social Security benefits. You must pay Social Security taxes on any income earned while taking benefits, either early or full benefits. Age 65 is also the point at which you begin receiving Medicare benefits.

How much money will Luke and Sarah need beyond their Social Security benefits of $2,226 a month to fund their retirement? If we use the Retirement Equation, we have a Social Security income of $26,712 per year. If we subtract that amount from their current annual budget of $65,608, we get an annual deficit of $38,896 a year or $3,241 per month. To maintain their desired standard of living, Luke and Sarah have to somehow add $38,896 a year to fund their desired retirement income needs, or they need to cut expenses. Take a look at the equation figures below:

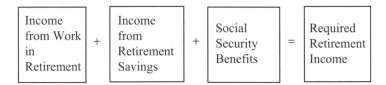

Or, for our current example of Luke and Sarah's plan:

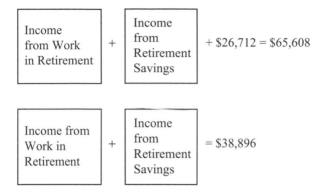

| Income from Work in Retirement | + | Income from Retirement Savings | + $26,712 = $65,608 |

| Income from Work in Retirement | + | Income from Retirement Savings | = $38,896 |

Taxes on Social Security

It should be noted that Social Security benefit payments can be taxed if you report enough combined income. The Social Security Web site indicates the following:

If you and your spouse have a combined income that is:

1. Between $32,000 and $44,000, you may have to pay income tax on 50 percent of your Social Security benefits.
2. If your combined income is more than $44,000, up to 85 percent of your Social Security benefits may be taxable.

Remember that after you retire, unless you're working, you won't be paying Social Security tax, Medicare tax, or contributing to an employer retirement plan. That frees up 15–20 percent.

▓ Summary

At this point, we've started to complete the Retirement Equation with two components: the budget (desired) and Social Security benefits.

| Income from Work in Retirement | + | Income from Retirement Savings | + | Social Security Benefits | = | Required or Desired Retirement Income |

Or, for our current example of Luke and Sarah's plan:

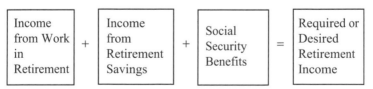

| Income from Work in Retirement | + | Income from Retirement Savings | + $26,712 = $65,608 |

Luke and Sarah still need to balance their Retirement Equation so the sum of the left side is equal to or greater than their desired income requirements on the right side of the equation. The next chapter will discuss ways to make up shortfalls between your Social Security benefits and costs.

■ References

American Association of Retired Persons. 2007. State-by-State Long-term Health Care Costs. http://www.aarp.org/family/caregiving/articles/state-by-state_longterm.html.

Bureau of Labor Statistics. 2008. U.S. Department of Labor, Bureau of Labor Statistics, Consumer Price Index All Urban Consumers, U.S. City Average. ftp://ftp.bls.gov/pub/special.requests/cpi/cpiai.txt.

Clements, Jonathan. "Pay off your mortgage before your retirement." *Wall Street Journal*, October 12, 2004, http://www.realestatejournal.com/buysell/mortgages/20041012-clements.html.

Employee Benefit Research Institute. 2004. Issue Brief No. 271 July 2004. Health Care Expenses in Retirement and the Use of Health Savings Accounts. By Paul Fronstin and Dallas Salisbury, EBRI, and Jack VanDerhei, Temple University and EBRI Fellow.

Employee Benefit Research Institute. 2008. Issue Brief No. 317 May 2008. Savings Needed to Fund Health Insurance and Health Care Expenses in Retirement: Findings from a Simulation Model. By Paul Fronstin and Dallas Salisbury, EBRI, and Jack VanDerhei, Temple University and EBRI Fellow.

Tully, Shawn. "Real Estate: Buy, Sell, or Hold?" *Fortune*, November 7, 2007, http://money.cnn.com/2007/11/06/real_estate/home_prices.fortune/index.htm.

U.S. Census Bureau. 2007. http://factfinder.census.gov/servlet/GRTTable?_bm=y&geo_id=01000US&_box_head_nbr=R2513&-ds_name=ACS_2007_1YR_G00_&-redoLog=false&-format=US-30&-mt_name=ACS_2006_EST_G00_R2513_US30.

6 ▪ ▪ ▪

Creating Income from Your Retirement Savings

The typical American retires at age 63. Those who are fortunate enough to have traditional pensions, retiree health insurance, and fully loaded 401(k) accounts are in great shape. For those who don't have sufficient savings and pension plans, the primary option is to work three more years or until Social Security begins to reach full benefits. The Congressional Budget Office estimates that in 2004, a middle-income, married couple would need to have saved $550,000 to retire at age 62 without a reduced standard of living. That amount drops to $325,000 if they retire at age 66, and to $130,000 if they can hold out until 70 (Brandon, 2008).

▪ Luke and Sarah Consider Options to Fund Their Retirement

As we noted in the previous chapter, Luke and Sarah have a $38,896 short-fall even with their Social Security benefits. Fortunately, they've been wise enough to balance their Social Security benefits with the following 401(k) retirement and investment accounts.

1. Luke: 401(k) retirement account: $135,000
2. Sarah: 401(k) retirement account: $150,000
3. Joint Investment Account: $205,000
4. Emergency Cash Fund: $ 36,000
   Total Savings: $526,000

While $526,000 might seem like a great deal of money, Luke and Sarah will need to make that money grow and last them for 20–30 years or more in their retirement.

What can Luke and Sarah do with their $526,000 in savings to make up the $38,896 shortfall after Social Security benefits? Do they have enough saved to cover their desired retirement expenses, keep pace with inflation, and not run out of money? While we have no idea how long Luke or Sarah will live, whether or not they will have significant health problems, or what the rate of inflation will be during their retirement, there are still numerous income distribution strategies that they can use. For our purposes we'll discuss two major options.

▦ Option 1: A Safe Withdrawal Rate

The most common method for generating income in retirement is by making regular withdrawals from a portfolio of investments (more on investments and growing your money in a later chapter). If Luke and Sarah take too much money out in the earlier years of retirement, they'll likely run out of money toward the end of their retirement, or need to drastically reduce spending. What Luke and Sarah need is a safe, fixed rate of withdrawal that can be increased for inflation each year while protecting them from running out of money.

Bengen (1994) first suggested a safe withdrawal rate (SWR) that would fund retirement income, increase each year to offset inflation, yet have a 90 percent chance of funding a full 30 years of retirement from a portfolio of 60 percent stocks and 40 percent bonds. The safe withdrawal rate is 4 percent and is adjusted by 3 percent each year thereafter for inflation. For example, $1,000,000 in investments would generate $40,000 the first year of retirement and $41,200 the second year to cover an anticipated rate of inflation of 3 percent (Bengen, 1994).

The 4 percent safe withdrawal rule is a popular strategy, used by most retirement specialists and brokers because it's easy for the retiree and planners to understand and implement (AARP, 2008; T. Rowe Price, 2008; Vanguard Group, 2008). Several other studies have been published that suggest that a higher rate of initial withdrawals is possible, but those methods are generally more complex and outside the scope of this book. For the sake of simplicity, we too will use the 4 percent rule to estimate the assets needed to fund retirement income requirements. As we will see, a 4 percent safe withdrawal plan will only partially cover Luke and Sarah's retirement needs.

▪ Option 2: Creating Your Own Pension

According to a 2007 Employee Benefits Research Institute report, only 10 percent of workers had a defined benefit, commonly known as a "traditional" pension plan. Only 27 percent of workers had a combination of a traditional pension and a 401(k)-type plan (Employee Benefit Research Institute, 2007). Traditional pension plans have declined as company and plan sponsors attempt to control costs and funding volatility and face additional pressures from increased regulatory burdens and increased life expectancies of their pensioners. While very few retirees can rely on a regular pension check from their employer, they can buy their own pension check from an insurance company in the form of an immediate annuity. An immediate annuity is an insurance policy, issued only by life insurance companies, which, in exchange for a sum of money, guarantees that the insurance company will make a series of payments to the purchaser of the annuity.

Immediate annuities can take several forms—the most basic is a single life annuity followed by a joint with survivor annuity. A single life immediate annuity will guarantee a regular pension check to a single person until their death, whether that is in 10 or 50 years. This is the least-expensive annuity. A joint annuity with survivor benefits will guarantee a regular income to joint annuity holders, typically spouses or a retiree and their beneficiary, for the life of both annuity holders. For an additional cost, the annuity provider can adjust the income checks each year for inflation calculated by the CPI-U or a rate specified by the retiree. The best example of an annuity is the Social Security benefit system.

The key advantage to immediate annuities is that the insurance company guarantees the income payments. This is essential because retirees are living longer; baby boomers can expect retirement to last 30 years or more. One of the biggest retirement fears reported is the possibility of outliving one's assets. The Employee Benefit Research Institute reports that only 29 percent of retirees are very confident that they will have enough money to live comfortably throughout their retirement years (Employee Benefit Research Institute, 2008). An immediate annuity can ensure that a retiree's available savings will last through their entire retirement years.

There are disadvantages to an immediate annuity. Once an annuity is purchased and payments begin, the retiree cannot sell the annuity easily to regain access to the cash used to purchase the annuity. Thus, the retiree loses control over that asset. The cost of the annuity can rise rapidly as benefits are added, such as adding survivor benefits and inflation adjustments. A 65-year-old retiree can expect to pay at least 30 percent more for an inflation-adjusted annuity. In addition, the payout amounts for an immediate annuity are highly dependent on the current interest rate environment.

The following table outlines the approximate cost of an immediate annuity. All data are from the Vanguard Lifetime Income Program online Instant Quote form accessed November 2008.

1) Immediate Annuity Cost for $1,000 Monthly Income Payment:

   (a) Male, 65, Single Life: $127,521
   (b) Female, 65, Single Life: $137,008
   (c) Joint Annuity, both 65, 100% Survivor Benefits: $153,546

2) Annuity Cost of $1,000 Monthly Payments with Annual Inflation Adjustments:

   (a) Male, 65, Single Life: $163,343
   (b) Female, 65, Single Life: $179,079
   (c) Joint Annuity, both 65, 100% Survivor Benefits: $207,436

For comparison, the same information was entered in Fidelity's Guaranteed Income Estimator (http://personal.fidelity.com/personal/annuities/) and Fidelity's quote for a 65-year-old male was $146,047 or $18,526 more for the same $1,000 of monthly income.

Immediate annuities are best for younger retirees because they will probably have ample time to recover the cost of the annuity. A retiree who is 80 years old obviously has less time than a 65-year-old to enjoy the full financial benefits of an immediate annuity.

Historically, many financial experts have not viewed annuities favorably because of unscrupulous sales practices and the very high sales commissions that were hidden within the annuity cost. Fortunately, Vanguard offers annuities through AIG Insurance without any additional sales charges, available directly to an individual investor at www.vanguard.com. If your financial advisor or insurance agent tries to offer you another annuity, be assertive and ask how much they are being paid to do so, and why their annuity is better than those offered commission-free through Vanguard.

Another option is a relatively new product called income-replacement funds or managed-payout funds. These funds are usually a portfolio of mutual funds and pay out a certain amount each month for a specified number of years. However, unlike an immediate annuity purchased from an insurance company, the income payments are not guaranteed. These income payments may fluctuate depending on the balance of the underlying mutual funds. These managed payout funds are an excellent example of when it pays to read the fine print and to truly understand the risks and rewards of using them to generate your income.

▪ Funding Luke and Sarah's Retirement Income

To continue with our example of Luke and Sarah, we know the following about their financial situation:

1. Retirement Income:

   a. Retirement Expenses (including taxes): $65,608
   b. Social Security Benefits: $26,712
   c. Income needed to fund retirement = $38,896

2. Retirement Savings:

   a. Luke: 401(k) retirement account: $135,000
   b. Sarah: 401(k) retirement account: $150,000
   c. Joint Investment Account: $205,000
   d. Emergency Cash Fund: $ 36,000
        Total Savings: $526,000

▪ Option 1: Safe Withdrawal Rate

Luke and Sarah have $526,000 between their two individual retirement accounts, the joint investment account, and their emergency cash fund. They would prefer to keep the emergency cash fund separate. They could invest $490,000 in a diversified portfolio of 60 percent stocks and 40 percent bonds and safely withdraw 4 percent for their first year of retirement. As you can see below, this provides $19,600 for the first year of retirement.

Assets Available to Invest: $490,000
4% Safe Withdrawal Amount: × 4% = $ 19,600

The results of a safe withdrawal rate of 4 percent are less than half of their retirement income shortfall. If they added the $36,000 in the emergency fund to their investment portfolio, it would only increase the annual safe withdrawal by $1,440. If they included the emergency cash fund and increased the rate of withdrawal to 5 percent, increasing the chances of outliving their assets, the annual withdrawal would still only be $26,300—or $17,800 short of their anticipated retirement needs.

To make the safe withdrawal strategy work, Luke and Sarah would need to cut $23,060 from their yearly retirement budget or save an additional $576,500 to fund their retirement needs, for a net investment savings of $1,103,000 or more than double what they have in investment savings at present.

Retirement Equation:

| Income from Work in Retirement | + | Cash Flow from $490,000 at 4% SWR | + $26,712 = $65,608 |

Or:

| Income from Work in Retirement | + $19,600 + $26,712 = $46,312 < $65,608 |

If they were to utilize the safe withdrawal method for funding their retirement, Luke and Sarah would definitely need to find additional income, probably finding additional work while in retirement.

■ Option 2: Immediate annuity

Luke and Sarah could also create their own pension by purchasing an immediate annuity from an insurance company. The immediate annuity would guarantee regular cash flow and place the burden of protecting assets against inflation in the hands of the insurance company.

> Immediate Annuity No Inflation Adjustment
> Annual Income (paid monthly): $ 38,896
> Joint Annuity, 100% Survivor Benefit
> Approximate annuity premium: $506,179

> Immediate Annuity with Inflation Adjustment
> Annual Income (paid monthly): $ 38,896
> Joint Annuity, inflation adjusted 100% Survivor Benefit
> Approximate annuity premium: $680,777

Both annuity premium quotes are still beyond the reach of Luke and Sarah's retirement assets, and they still need to protect those assets against inflation. Using the Vanguard online annuity quote calculator again, we can determine what annual income, adjusted for inflation, their assets could purchase.

> Immediate Annuity with Inflation Adjustment
> Assets available for annuity: $490,000

Joint Annuity, inflation adjusted 100% Survivor Benefit.
Approximate Annual Income: $29,146

Using all of their available assets to purchase the annuity still
would not cover their retirement income needs and adjust for inflation, but it certainly gets them closer.

Another annuity option to consider is to reduce the amount of the sur-
viving spouse benefit—that is, if Luke were to die before Sarah, Sarah
would continue to receive the full annuity amount under the 100 percent
survivor benefit. If that survivor benefit were cut in half to a 50 percent
survivor benefit:

Immediate Annuity with Inflation Adjustment
Assets available for annuity: $ 490,000
Joint Annuity, inflation adjusted 50% Survivor Benefit.
Approximate Annual Income: $32,213

Retirement Equation with Annuity:

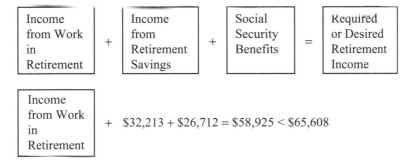

Even reducing the annuity survivor benefits to 50 percent does not balance the Retirement Equation, leaving the remaining options to working
in retirement or reducing the income required.

Clearly, neither option, nor a combination of the two, will balance Luke
and Sarah's Retirement Equation and provide their desired retirement
income. Luke and Sarah will need to make some decisions—they currently
have several luxury expenses they could cut until their mortgage is paid
off, or they could also continue to work full time for a couple more years.
We'll explore these options further in the next chapters.

▪ A Quick Estimator for Necessary Retirement Assets

Once you have determined what your retirement budget is, you could use
a close approximation using the examples and numbers we have outlined

herein. Instead of redoing each calculation for Option 1 and Option 2 with each change you make to your retirement budget or retirement savings, use the following estimators:

Amount of Savings Required for each $1,000 of Yearly Income

a. Option 1 (Safe Withdrawal Rate): $25,000
b. Option 2 (Annuity, Inflation Adjustment): $13,000 (at 2008 interest rates)

Using these formulas, you would need a total of $625,000 in savings to produce $25,000 a year for 25 years using the safe withdrawal method, and $325,000 to purchase $25,000 a year through an inflation-adjusted annuity.

Why the difference? And why would someone not choose the annuity option? For some, there will not be an option. However, the advantage to having saved more and being able to live on less than what your investments can generate leaves several options on the table. With the annuity option, there is no remaining cash savings; perhaps all of your retirement assets are turned into a steady stream of monthly paychecks. What if there is an immediate need for significant cash, either for medical or other lifestyle needs? There will need to be continued savings from the annuity paychecks to cover the unexpected. The safe withdrawal method will still leave the balance of the retirement accounts available at any time for access should the need arise.

A second key difference is leaving a legacy to your beneficiaries. This doesn't necessarily mean leaving your wealth to children, but to any charitable cause of your choosing. Purchasing an immediate annuity with only an inflation adjustment does not leave anything to a beneficiary at the time of your death unless you purchase an additional rider that provides for that benefit or you purchase additional whole life insurance specifically for that purpose. However, if you can live within the means provided by the returns generated by your retirement accounts, then you not only have access to cash in an emergency, but you also have the option of leaving a legacy behind to the beneficiaries of your choosing.

▨ References

American Association of Retired Persons. 2008. "Managing money in retirement: Make your money last." http://www.aarp.org/money/financial_planning/sessionseven/managing_money_in_retirement.html (accessed February 26, 2008).

Bengen, William P. 1994. "Determining withdrawal rates using historical data." *Journal of Financial Planning* 7(4): 171–80.

Brandon, Emily. 2008. "How Much Longer Will Boomers Need to Work?" *U.S. News and World Report*, August, 11, 2008, http://www.usnews.com/articles/

business/retirement/2008/08/11/how-much-longer-will-boomers-need-to-work.html

Employee Benefit Research Institute. 2007. Facts from EBRI: Retirement Trends in the United States Over the Past Quarter Century, June 2007.

Employee Benefit Research Institute. 2008. Employee Benefit Research Institute Issue Brief No. 316, April 2008.

T. Rowe Price. 2008. Investment Guidance & Tools: Retirement Planning: Living in Retirement: A withdrawal rule of thumb. http://www.troweprice.com/common/index3/0,3011,lnp percent253D10014 percent2526cg percent253D1210 percent2526pgid percent253D7549,00.html (accessed February 26, 2008).

Vanguard. 2008. Planning & Education: Retirement: Managing Your Retirement: Tap Your Assets: Determine how much you can withdraw. https://personal.vanguard.com/us/planningeducation/retire ment/PEdRetTapDetermine WDContent.jsp (accessed February 26, 2008).

7 ▪ ▪ ▪

How to Make Your Numbers Work

The point of the Retirement Equation is that it must balance. For some, the right side of the equation will be *Required* Retirement Income, and for others it may be *Available* Retirement Income. While essentially the same, we all will have our Required Retirement Income needs those costs for housing, utilities, and health care that we simply cannot live without. For those retirees who have significant savings and may even be fortunate enough to have a pension, Available retirement income may far exceed Required retirement income. In the previous chapter, the couple in the example found that they didn't have enough assets to cover the income needs for their estimated retirement budget. They are faced with making the following important decisions and questions:

1. How can they reduce their budget?
2. Should they continue to work for one or two more years?
3. Would a combination of the safe withdrawal rate and an immediate annuity stretch their assets further?

After reviewing their budget, Luke and Sarah realized that they had a sizable emergency cash reserve, and felt they didn't need to continue to add to that account, saving $3,600 per year. They also decided that they

Table 7.1
Luke and Sara's Revised Retirement Budget

Category	Description	Annual	Monthly
Housing	Property Taxes	$ 3,000	$ 250
	Insurance	$ 1,200	$ 100
	Heating, Electricity, etc.	$ 6,000	$ 500
	Phones	$ 940	$ 78
	Maintenance	$ 2,500	$ 208
	Home Supplies	$ 600	$ 50
	Miscellaneous	$ 500	$ 60
	Mortgage / Rent	$ 7,200	$ 600
Car	Insurance	$ 600	$ 50
	Gas	$ 1,200	$ 100
	License	$ 120	$ 10
	Maintenance	$ 360	$ 30
	Payment	$ 2,400	$ 200
Food	Groceries	$ 4,800	$ 400
Pets	Food	$ 240	$ 20
	License	$ 24	$ 2
	Vet	$ 100	$ 8
Personal	Healthcare	$ 9,000	$ 750
	Clothing	$ 500	$ 42
	Newspaper	$ 60	$ 5
	Miscellaneous	$ 1,200	$ 100
	Health Club	$ 960	$ 80
Charity		$ 500	$ 42
Luxuries	Travel	$ 4,000	$ 333
	Entertainment	$ 2,400	$ 200
	Gifts	$ 500	$ 42
	Personal	$ 1,200	$ 100
	Other	$ 1,200	$ 100
Savings	Emergency fund	$ 0	$ 0
Total Before-Tax Income Required		$53,304	$ 4,442
10% Income Tax		$ 5,330	$ 444
Total Required Retirement Income		$58,634	$ 4,886

would be willing to reduce some other luxury items, like travel, and would keep one car much longer to save on payments. Their revised retirement budget is shown in Table 7.1.

Even after reducing luxury items from their budget, housing, cars, and health care still make up the majority of their budget, and those numbers can't be reduced easily. Still, they were able to cut $6,974 from the spending plan. Using a shortened version of the Retirement Equation and with a little rearrangement:

Required or Desired Retirement Income		Social Security Benefits		Income from Retirement Savings
	−		=	
$58,634	−	$26,712	=	$31,922

Assets Needed to Generate $31,922 the First Year of Retirement

a. Safe Withdrawal Rate of 4%: $798,050
b. Immediate Annuity, Dual Life, 100% Survivor Benefits, Inflation Adjusted: $558,870

Both options still surpass Luke and Sarah's assets. Luke and Sarah are ready to retire, but neither wants to retire and not be able to afford a few luxuries they feel make retirement worth working for. If both Luke and Sarah worked for one additional year, they would be able to accumulate one more year of assets. In addition, by delaying retirement until they're 66, their Social Security benefits would increase by 8 percent (www.social-security.gov/retire2/delayret.htm). If Luke and Sarah retire at 65, their benefits would amount to $26,712. If they wait one year, their benefits increase $2,138 to $28,850, annually. Let's see how this added amount affects their shortfall:

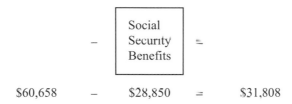

		Social Security Benefits		
	−		=	
$60,658	−	$28,850	=	$31,808

Note that we added an inflation amount to the income required, but we did not include inflation on the amount needed for the mortgage and car payments. Those payments are fixed and will not increase with inflation.

Even with the $2,138 in additional Social Security benefits, Luke and Sarah still face almost a $32,000 shortfall to fund retirement. It would take $795,200 in assets and a 4 percent withdrawal rate to cover the $31,808 shortfall, but only $537,553 to provide the same amount of money in an immediate annuity with dual life, 100 percent survivor benefits, and inflation adjustment to fund the same amount of money.

If Luke and Sarah continued to save during their last year of employment, the numbers start to improve even more. If they were to save 15 percent of their combined income of $90,000, that would give them an additional $13,500 of assets, not including any interest earned. Luke and Sarah would also have one more year to have their existing assets increase in value before they needed to access those funds. We'll assume that those assets gain only 5 percent per year.

New Asset Values after Waiting One Year to Retire
Existing Savings at Age 65:	$526,000
Interest Earned at 5%:	$26,300
Additional Savings, one more year of employment:	$13,500
New total savings, retiring at 66:	$565,800

By delaying retirement one year and reducing some of their expenses, they've managed to not only increase their savings by 7.5 percent, but also to pay one more year of their mortgage and car loans with their salaries. And they increase their income from Social Security. This leaves them with additional options for funding their retirement income. After waiting one year to retire, Luke and Sarah can afford to create their own pension income with their assets and leave $28,247 in savings.

Retirement Equation after One Additional Year of Work:

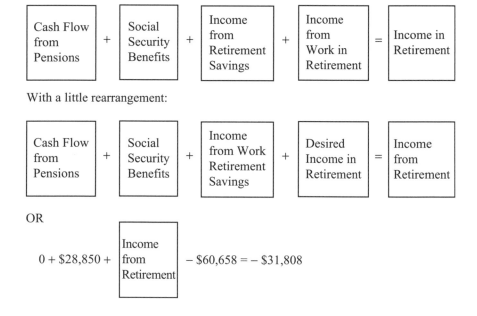

With a little rearrangement:

OR

Annuity required to fund $31,808 shortfall = $537,553

Working one additional year has accomplished several things. It allowed for one additional year of savings; one additional year of not withdrawing funds from savings, allowing savings to grow; increased Social Security benefits; and ultimately, balanced Luke and Sarah's Retirement Equation.

Combining an Immediate Annuity with SWR

After waiting one year to retire, Luke and Sarah can afford to create their own pension income with their assets and leave $28,247 in savings. However, they'd like to investigate one more option that could leave more room financially for emergencies or other life changes. Luke and Sarah can afford an immediate annuity now after working one more year, which will guarantee them a consistent monthly income for both of their lives. However, this option only leaves them with $28,247 left in cash savings

Luke and Sarah could use guaranteed income sources to fund only those expenses that are nondiscretionary. Looking back at their revised budget, the nondiscretionary part of their budget is approximately $41,000 before tax or $45,100 with a 10 percent income tax.

Let's review their numbers another way:

Nondiscretionary Spending:	$45,100
Social Security Benefits Received:	−$28,850
Shortfall for Nondiscretionary Spending:	$16,250

Using the immediate annuity income calculator as before, to produce $16,250 with an annuity with 100 percent survivor benefits and annual inflation adjustments, the upfront premium cost would be $284,545.

Luke and Sarah's remaining assets to invest would be:

Beginning retirement and investment assets:	$565,800
Cost of Immediate Annuity to fund Nondiscretionary Spending:	−$284,545
Remaining assets to cover discretionary spending:	$281,255

At this point, Luke and Sarah have covered their nondiscretionary spending with two sources of guaranteed income: Social Security and an immediate annuity. Plus, they now have $281,255 of investable assets to fund their nondiscretionary spending or to cover any life emergencies. In addition, when their mortgage has been paid off, an additional $7,200 per year will be made available from their guaranteed income sources.

How should they manage the remaining $281,255? There is a multitude of ways, but we'll consider two simple cases. The first would be to manage it with the safe withdrawal strategy:

Remaining Assets:	$281,255
4% SWR:	× 4%
Annual safe withdrawal:	$ 11,250

However, if we look at this within the Retirement Equation again:

Social Security + Immediate Annuity + SWR = Retirement Income
$28,850 + $16,250 + $11,250 = $56,350 < $58,634

Luke and Sarah would need to withdraw $13,534 each year from their invested retirement assets to make their Retirement Equation balance with their desired income requirements. This is 4.81 percent of their assets.

Is this rate of withdrawal too much? Some may argue yes, as it's greater than the safe withdrawal rate of 4 percent. On the other hand, Luke and Sarah's nondiscretionary spending is guaranteed, and more of that income will be available once their mortgage is paid off. Each case will be different, and this scenario is an excellent example of when to utilize the services of a financial planner to develop a plan to ensure that those remaining assets are protected and invested correctly and that those assets produce the income necessary to enjoy retirement.

Each retiree's income needs later in life will vary dramatically. It could be argued that a retiree's income requirements will plateau at some point as they take fewer and fewer vacations, eat out less, and are generally less active. By assuming that income requirements don't change, Luke and Sarah will ensure that they do indeed have enough to support themselves throughout retirement. They may at some point be less active and spend less on entertainment and travel, but they may in turn need that income to hire additional outside help to maintain their home or provide some in-home medical care, which could allow them to remain independent longer.

■ Summary

Luke and Sarah have developed a strategy that includes working one more year and decreasing some expenses, which will give them an acceptable level of guaranteed income both from Social Security and an immediate annuity. In addition, they are able to keep a significant portion of their retirement savings available to invest in assets, such as mutual funds, which will allow them to grow those assets and withdraw a portion each year to keep pace with inflation.

Luke and Sarah have developed a good financial plan for their retirement income needs, but they need to remember that many things can change, and they should revisit their financial plan every few years and make adjustments as necessary.

8 ▪ ▪ ▪

Options to Increase Retirement Income

As we found out in the last chapter, delaying collecting Social Security benefits can add 8 percent per year to your benefits if you were born in 1943 or later. In addition, delaying retirement even one year can add up as retirement savings aren't tapped for income and additional savings can be added and invested.

T. Rowe Price recently published a report (first in *The Price Report*, 2008; republished in the *American Association of Individual Investors Journal*, 2008) that found similar results as we did for Luke and Sarah's case. The T. Rowe Price study found that those approaching retirement can improve their income and financial security based on four general factors that are within the retirees' control. Those are:

1. When they stop working.
2. When they start taking Social Security benefits.
3. How they manage withdrawals from their retirement savings.
4. How they allocate their assets.

The first two are the biggest factors in determining how much the retiree will have saved and what level of income they will have when they do quit work. The second two factors will impact the sustainability of their retirement savings and have been covered previously in sections on safe withdrawal rates. The T. Rowe Price study confirms that a 4 percent withdrawal rate from a portfolio of 60 percent stocks and 40 percent bonds has a 90 percent chance of success after 30 years.

■ Working Longer

As we noted in Chapter 2, there is a good deal of evidence that older adults who regularly work after retirement enjoy better health and live longer, thanks to stimulating environments and a sense of purpose (Zedlewski and Butrica, 2007). Calvo (2006) found that paid work for older adults improves health. Dhaval, Rashad, and Spasojevic (2006) found that complete retirement without work decreases physical and mental health.

While this option generally is sometimes unappealing to those approaching retirement, as we found in Luke and Sarah's example, working one additional year and cutting a few luxury expenses helped bridge the financial gap required for their retirement. As Luke and Sarah discovered, working one more year delayed withdrawing funds from their savings to cover expenses (allowing those assets to grow) and added an additional 15 percent of their salaries to their retirement savings.

The T. Rowe Price study found that a 62-year-old who continued to work full-time could expect to increase his or her retirement income from investments about 7 percent per additional year worked. If that same pre-retiree worked an additional three years and contributed 15 percent each year to their retirement investments, he would expect to increase his retirement income from investments by 22 percent, or as high as 39 percent if he worked an additional five years. Their study found that working an additional five years and saving 25 percent of annual earnings could increase retirement income by as much as 50 percent.

■ Delaying Social Security

Luke and Sarah increased their Social Security benefits 8 percent by delaying their retirement for one year, as would anyone else who was born in 1943 or later. If we use the example of Luke and Sarah again, but assume that they're 62 (the first year they can claim benefits) and use their combined income of $90,000, the impact of delaying retirement is outlined in the following table. The data are from the Social Security Administration Web site Quick Calculator and are in today's dollars.

Delaying receiving benefits clearly results in a higher income in today's dollars. When adjusted for inflation, using the Social Security Administration data, beginning benefits at age 70 would be 135 percent higher than

Table 8.1
Delaying Social Security Benefits Increases Retirement Income

Age Benefits Begin	Annual Social Security Benefits	% Increase over taking benefits at 62
62	$17,028	—
63	$18,240	7.1%
64	$19,932	17.1%
65	$21,648	27.1%
66	$23,400	37.4%
67	$25,476	49.6%
68	$27,588	62.0%
69	$29,712	74.5%
70	$31,872	87.2%

if the couple retired at age 62. If one took benefits at 66 and lived to age 85, the total benefits, excluding cost-of-living increases, would be $468,000. The same person taking benefits at 70 and living to 85 would receive total benefits of $478,125, excluding cost-of-living adjustments. You can see that the longer you wait to take Social Security benefits the more overall income you get. Taking the same example and comparing 66–90 and 70–90, the total benefits for the 66-year-old who lives to be 90 is $585,000, excluding cost-of-living increases, while the person taking benefits at 70 and living to age 90 would receive total benefits of $637,440, a substantial difference of $52,440.

The T. Rowe Price study found that a 62-year-old who delayed retirement until 65 and continued to save and invest 15 percent of his income would see more than a 20 percent increase in combined retirement income. A 65-year-old who waited until 67, also saving 15 percent of income, would increase his total retirement income by almost 20 percent.

There are advantages and disadvantages to taking Social Security benefits earlier or later. By taking benefits sooner, a retiree could withdraw less from retirement investments, allowing those accounts to continue to grow. On the other hand, if the retiree can afford it, Social Security benefits can act as a hedge against longevity. Delaying taking Social Security benefits clearly decreases the possibility of outliving one's assets.

Other Ways to Bridge the Financial Gap

We offer the following suggestions for alternative ways of bridging the gap between what you need in financial resources to retire and to be true to your actual needs and what you actually have.

Mortgages

As we can see from Luke and Sarah's example, their mortgage added at a minimum $92,000 to their required savings for retirement. We still feel that being mortgage-free is one of the biggest bonuses for retirement-income planning. If Luke and Sarah had made one additional monthly payment per year from the inception of their mortgage, they would have cut roughly six years of the life of their mortgage and would only have an additional four years to pay on it during retirement. They would also be saving about $30,000 in interest payments that could in turn be applied toward their retirement savings.

Taking equity out of one's home is an option to cover debt and to fund retirement expenses, but it prolongs the life of the mortgage. Our position is that you should pay off a home mortgage as soon as possible to lower your overall debt. For some retirees, another option is a reverse mortgage. With reverse mortgages, home equity is converted into a monthly payment to the homeowner, a one-time lump-sum payment, or as a line of credit to be used as needed.

Using the AARP reverse mortgage calculator (http://www.rmaarp.com/), a retiree age 62 would get a monthly payment of $592 on a home appraised at $200,000 from the federally insured "Home Equity Conversion Mortgage" (HECM). Over 30 years a reverse mortgage could net a retiree $213,120 if taken in monthly payments, or a one time lump sum at the time of loan closing of $105,674.

Remember that a reverse mortgage is different from a regular mortgage in that when you sell your home or no longer use it for your primary residence, you or your estate will repay the cash you received from the reverse mortgage, plus interest and other fees, to the lender. The remaining equity in your home, if any, belongs to you or to your heirs. None of your other assets will be affected by HUD's reverse mortgage loan. This debt will never be passed along to the estate or heirs. The amount you can borrow depends on your age, the current interest rate, and the appraised value of your home or FHA's mortgage limits for your area, whichever is less. Generally, the more valuable your home is, the older you are, and the lower the interest rate of your reverse mortgage, the more you can borrow.

Is there a downside to reverse mortgages? Yes. Some unscrupulous people have gotten into the reverse mortgage business. For that reason, it's best to deal with lenders who are authorized to lend you money from federally insured programs such as the "Home Equity Conversion Mortgage" we discussed earlier. If you don't understand reverse mortgages, be sure to read up on them or discuss them in detail with a lender. Remember that the amount you owe on a reverse mortgage grows over time. Interest is charged on the outstanding balance and added to the amount you owe each month. That means that your total debt increases over time as loan funds are advanced to you and interest accrues on the loan. It's possible that when you or your heirs sell the home you may not be able to get its true worth because the principle and interest you owe on the reverse mortgage may be more than you can make in profit from the sale of your home. In general, reverse mortgages are, or should be, a last resort for those who have depleted all other resources. Reverse mortgages should not be used as a method of accessing cash to invest in riskier investments. The costs associated with a reverse mortgage are generally much greater than the returns available with other investments, and those investments may not be guaranteed. Furthermore, if there is sufficient equity in the home, then a home equity line of credit (HELOC) is likely to provide access to needed cash at a much lower cost and at terms more easily understood by the borrower.

Credit cards

This applies to everyone, but especially to those who need to save more for retirement: If you can't afford it, don't buy it. It is difficult to save money for retirement or to pay off a mortgage early if credit card balances can't be paid in full each month. While we recognize that a good deal of seniors' credit card debt is related to paying for essentials, including health care, credit card debt among seniors is a serious problem that causes great stress for many retirees.

Nearly one-third of all senior citizens in the United States carry credit card balances (Todorova, 2007). Within that group, the average debt is $4,041—an 89 percent increase over the past decade. For all age groups, the average debt increased by 53 percent over this same time period. The debt increase is particularly heavy during the first years of retirement when people aged 65 to 69 found their credit card balances growing by 217 percent, to $5,844. Because the debt amounts in this article were self-reported by consumers rather than creditors, the real numbers could be much higher.

Adding to credit card debt is the number of older adult bankruptcies. Todorova (2007) reports that the rate at which retirees are filing for bankruptcy has more than doubled over the past 10 years, and retirees are now the fastest-growing segment of bankrupted Americans. An Associated Press article reports that in 1991, the 55-plus age group accounted for about 8 percent of bankruptcy filers (AP, 2008). By 2007, filers 55 and over accounted for 22 percent. Although each age group under 55 saw double-digit percentage drops in their bankruptcy filing rates over the survey period, older Americans saw remarkable increases. The filing rate per thousand people ages 55–64 was up 40 percent; among 65- to 74-year-olds it increased 125 percent; and among the 75-to-84-year-old set, it was up 433 percent.

Helping to explain the credit card crunch for seniors and the increasing number of bankruptcies, Haveman and colleagues (2005) found that about one-half of new retirees lack sufficient resources to permit them to maintain their estimated budgets in retirement. Even worse, the authors found that 25 percent of all new retirees have insufficient resources to allow even a near-poverty level of living during retirement.

The Employee Benefit Research Group confirms that elderly debt levels continue to rise. The EBRI reports that the oldest elderly incurred sharply higher debt levels between 1992 and 2004. The average debt for a family with head of household age 75 or older rose to $20,234 in 2004 from $7,769 in 1992. Housing debt has become a larger factor for families with a head of household age of 55 or older, increasing from 24 percent to 36 percent over the same time period. The EBRI (2006) found that the increase in debt was mainly due to homeowners refinancing their mortgages, cashing out equity in their homes, or facing rapidly increasing home values during 2001–2004 when buying a home.

Working part-time

It's true that work can be a physical and emotional stressor if the work done is menial, uncreative, or just plain physically taxing. The trick is to find work that not only offers the possibility of creativity, but also pays well enough for it to improve your financial picture. We know of many older adults who work a day or two a week or who get paid for what might otherwise be volunteer work because the pay provides a stronger sense of acceptance by a business or organization. Dr. Glicken, for example, teaches a day a week at Arizona State University, and while the pay is nominal, the pleasure of working with young, active, intellectually stimulating students is priceless.

Remember, you need to save between $18,000 and $25,000 to generate $1,000 of annual income. If a retiree can find part-time work or create work out of a current hobby, $10,000 in part-time income could reduce required savings by as much as $180,000. Granted, the part-time income may not be sustainable throughout 30 years of retirement, but the lowered draw from savings will create an added financial cushion. As an alternative, at the beginning of retirement, income from a part-time job or business could be used to delay receiving Social Security; the added benefits were clearly outlined previously.

Although it's true that some employers are rigid about work schedules and pay, Weckerle and Shultz (1999) correctly point out that many organizations recognize that older workers provide a positive work ethic that translates into more cost-effective employees. As that realization becomes more widely accepted, employers will not only offer more flexible part-time schedules, but also better pay. So don't give up on the possibility of finding well-paying and interesting part-time work because you've encountered some ageism in the past or reluctance to hire part-time workers. The fact is that older workers are often more conscientious, efficient, and loyal to organizations than younger workers.

An example

A 74-year-old friend of ours in Long Beach, California, continues to work two days a week for a physician's group where she does the billing, payroll, and benefits from her home. The added income allows her to keep her 401(k) investments untouched and growing to cover expenses when she can no longer work and to pay for some additional life pleasures such as traveling. She also says that the work keeps her challenged and that feeling needed is a strong incentive to be actively involved in life. She told us, "The worst thing for a retired person is to stop using his/her intellectual abilities. I don't feel old because I'm doing work a lot of people much younger than I am can't do. It's a strong message to myself that, 'kiddo, you still got it.'"

Another example

A doctor who retired after selling his long-time practice, found his savings to be limited, his medical insurance beyond Medicare nonexistent, and in general, too much time on his hands. Instead of going back to work in the medical profession, he went through the local school systems bus driver-training program. He now has a regular route with the school system, which he finds enjoyable and occupies enough time, but still allows him the same vacation schedule as the rest of the school system. Just as important, the bus driving provides him with additional income and health benefits, and after 10 years of driving, he can leave the school system and still be covered by the school system's health plan.

Monetizing your hobby

Work after retirement doesn't necessarily mean going to work for someone or doing what you did previously. It can be finding a way to make money from doing something that you already enjoy. Ideas include: house- and pet-sitting, selling items you make at craft fairs, maintaining gardens for others, or handyman work. Perhaps you can turn your success as a business owner into a small consulting service, turning your years of experience into a modest income. Others may find that spending the entire day on the golf course is their life's dream, and that the best way to achieve that is to get a job as a range master or working in the pro shop.

▪ Summary

Important points for planning your retirement income include being both creative and flexible. In any case, it is important to understand your starting point, what you need and what you have, and to work through a number of options to create the income you need.

If you're retiring with limited assets or just aren't ready to retire full-time, each additional dollar you make in retirement is one less dollar that you'll need to withdraw from your retirement savings. This not only takes the pressure off those savings, but it also allows each dollar to continue to grow, tax-free if in a qualified retirement plan. In addition, in the earlier example, one can turn work in retirement into a source of lifetime health care coverage.

■ References

Associated Press. 2008. "Associated Press Study: Bankruptcies soar for senior citizens." http://www.msnbc.msn.com/id/26427259.

Calvo, E. *Does Working Longer Make People Healthier and Happier? Work Opportunities for Older Americans*, Series 2. Chestnut Hill, MA: Center for Retirement Research, Boston College, 2006.

Dhaval, D., I. Rashad, and J. Spasojevic. 2006. The Effects of Retirement on Physical and Mental Health Outcomes. NBER Working Paper 12123. Cambridge, MA: NBER.

Employee Benefit Research Institute. 2006. Debt of the Elderly and Near Elderly 1992–2004. Employee Benefit Research Institute, Notes, September 2006, Vol. 27, No. 9.

Haveman, R., K. Holden, B. Wolfe, and S. Sherlund. 2005. "Do newly retired workers in the United States have sufficient resources to maintain well-being?" *Economic Inquiry* doi:10.1093/ei/cbj023 (ISSN 0095-2583) Advance Access publication, November 18, 2005, Vol. 44, No. 2, April 2006, 249–64.

T. Rowe Price. *The Price Report, Summer 2008*. Reprinted in *American Association of Individual Investors Journal*, August 2008.

Todorova, A. "The senior debt crisis." *SmartMoney Magazine*, February 12, 2007, http://www.smartmoney.com/consumer/index.cfm?story=20040311

Weckerle, J., and K. Shultz. 1999. "Influences on the bridge employment of older USA workers. Department of Psychology, California State University." *Journal of Occupational and Organizational Psychology* 72:317–20. Printed in Great Britain.

Zedlewski, S. R., and B. A. Butrica. 2007. *Are We Taking Full Advantage of Older Adults' Potential? The Retirement Project: Perspectives of Productive Aging*. The Urban Institute: 9.

9 ▪ ▪ ▪

Know Your Pension

In this chapter, we will focus on private company defined-benefit pension plans. While many plans appear to be healthy, some are in serious trouble, especially those instituted by private companies. Unlike a municipality or other government entity, private companies cannot tax their way out of a pension shortfall issue and are therefore more at risk than publicly funded pension plans. Even so, public pension plans are in serious difficulty as well. Writing in the *New York Times*, Williams Walsh (2003) reports that state and local pension funds have committed themselves to $375 billion more in benefits than they have funded. It is, along with failures of private pension plans, one of the most serious blows to retirees who thought they were in very good, even excellent, shape for retirement. Although we don't think this poses an immediate threat to public employees, the wise person must take into consideration that serious mistakes have been made in the funding of public and private pension plans, and you need to find out as much about the health of a plan as possible as you approach retirement.

In 1974, the Employee Retirement Income Security Act (ERISA) was passed into federal law. It governs private-sector retirement and health plans. ERISA established new, stringent requirements for private-sector defined-benefit pensions, and more importantly, it established the Pension

Benefit Guaranty Corporation (PBGC). The PBGC was created because private pensions can fail, either due to under funding (despite ERISA funding requirements) or the company declares bankruptcy. There is no readily available data for how many private pensions fail each year, but in 2003, approximately 150 pensions failed (Williams Walsh, 2003).

An employer can end a pension plan two ways: a standard termination or a distress termination (failure). A standard termination requires that the company show the PBGC that the plan has enough money to pay all benefits owed. At this point, the plan purchases an annuity from an insurance company or offers a lump-sum payout to the retiree.

A distress termination occurs when the company has not fully funded its pension plan. The employer must prove to a bankruptcy court or to the PBGC that the employer cannot remain in business unless the plan is terminated. At that point, the PBGC will take over payment of the plan benefits up to the legal limits (more on this shortly). The PBGC can also terminate a pension plan when it sees that it is in the interest of the plan participants to do so. This usually occurs if the PBGC determines that the plan does not have the funds necessary to pay benefits currently due.

How will you know if your plan is being terminated or failing? If a plan is undergoing a standard termination, the pension plan administrator must notify you in writing within 60 days of the termination date that the plan is ending. You will also receive a second letter, the Notice of Plan Benefits, describing the benefits you will receive. If the pension plan is failing and is terminated either by the company or the PBGC as a distress termination, the PBGC will begin communication with you after they have taken over administration of the pension plan. In either case, we feel that retirees who expect to or currently receive benefits from a private pension plan should contact their plan administrator or check with the PBGC to verify the status of the pension plan (PGBC Web site: www.pbgc.gov).

If your private-sector pension plan does fail, the PBGC will take over payment of the plan benefits to the retirees. When a pension fails, there are certain benefits the PBGC will cover but other benefits it won't cover. The PBGC guarantees the following:

1. Pension benefits at normal retirement age.
2. Most early retirement benefits.
3. Annuity benefits for survivors of plan participants.
4. Disability benefits.

The PBGC does not guarantee the following:

1. Health and welfare benefits.
2. Vacation pay.
3. Severance benefits.

4. Lump-sum death benefits for a death that occurs after the plan termination date.
5. Disability benefits for a disability that occurs after the plan's termination date.

In addition, there are legal limits to the benefits that the PBGC can pay out to retirees. For a 65-year-old retiree in 2008, the maximum legal limit is $51,750 a year for a straight-life annuity, or $46,575 a year for a joint annuity with a 50 percent survivor annuity. The following shows PBGC monthly limits by age at which a pension is taken for straight-life annuities and joint annuities with 50 percent survivor benefits:

PBGC Maximum Monthly Guarantees for 2008

Age	Straight-Life Annuity	2008 Joint with 50% Survivor Annuity
65	$4,312.50	$3,881.25
64	$4,010.63	$3,609.57
63	$3,708.75	$3,337.88
62	$3,406.88	$3,066.19
61	$3,105.00	$2,794.50
60	$2,803.13	$2,522.82
59	$2,630.63	$2,367.57
58	$2,458.13	$2,212.32
57	$2,285.63	$2,057.07
56	$2,113.13	$1,901.82
55	$1,940.63	$1,746.57
50	$1,509.38	$1,358.44
45	$1,078.13	$ 970.32

There are two very important points to note here. First, if you were planning your retirement expenses on expected benefits greater than the legal limits, you will have to adjust to those limits. If you were expecting $75,000 per year at retirement, the maximum you will receive is $51,750 if your plan fails. Second, if your plan is terminated, the PBGC does not guarantee any health care benefits that may have been part of your retirement benefits. As discussed, health care expenses are expected to be one of the biggest expenses in retirement.

We encourage those who are retiring now, or are retired with pension benefits, to utilize the resources of the PBGC and their plan administrator. Retirees who are proactive and informed will be prepared should they face any changes to their benefits due to plan terminations, standard or distressed.

You may also want to consider the following signs of trouble brewing for your pension plan as noted by Pullium Weston (2006):

1. Your company is in bankruptcy court or headed that way.
2. Your company's competitors are in bankruptcy court. This may suggest difficulties for most companies in a certain business or manufacturing sector.
3. Your company's credit is bad.
4. Your company is being sold.
5. Your plan is particularly generous. The fix for public and private pensions may well be to reduce benefits for new hires.
6. Your plan is in worse shape this year than it was last year.
7. Your plan's administrators, trustees, or auditors keep changing.
8. The plan's auditors are raising alarms that the pension plan is in trouble.
9. Former employees are having trouble getting their benefits.
10. Your plan won't give you answers. You can get many documents about your plan from the Labor Department, but if a plan won't answer questions, it is a certain sign of trouble.

▦ References

Pension Benefit Guaranty Corporation Web site, www.pbgc.gov.

Pullium Weston, Liz. "10 warning signs of pension peril." http://articles.money central.msn.com/RetirementandWills/CreateaPlan/10warningSignsOfPension Peril.aspx (accessed June 20, 2006).

Williams Walsh, Mary. "Failed Pensions: A Painful Lesson in Assumptions." *The New York Times*, November 12, 2003.

10 ▪ ▪ ▪

Investment Options and Finding Help

Many people approaching retirement age in 2008 have probably not changed jobs or careers very frequently, but it is a very different story for the youngest baby boomers. According to the Bureau of Labor Statistics (2008), the youngest baby boomers (born between 1957 and 1964) have held an average of 10.8 jobs (U.S. Bureau of Labor Statistics, 2008). With that many job changes, the number of retirement accounts that were opened, funded, and left behind is probably large.

Regardless of how many different employers or careers you may have had, even if you're not close to retirement, we recommend that you combine all of your retirement accounts into a single account. This will accomplish several things: it will give you a full accounting of all your retirement accounts; it will make management of those assets easier, and stray accounts won't be lost. Granted, some people may only collect one or two thousand dollars at a job they were at briefly, but those couple thousand add up over time, and growth rates compound these dollars to an even greater amount.

■ Combining Retirement Accounts

For those of you who are still in the workforce and are enrolled in your employer's qualified retirement plan, previous retirement accounts can be transferred into your new employer's plan. There are numerous retirement plan designations, depending on the type of employer. These include 401(k), 403(b), 457(f), Thrift Savings, Simple-IRAs and SEP-IRAs. Fortunately, instead of having multiple retirement account types, all qualified accounts can be combined. Your old 401(k) can be moved into a new 403(b), or the other way around. If you don't like your current retirement plan, or you are in the process of retiring, all qualified plans can be moved to a single Rollover IRA, which can also be combined with an existing traditional IRA.

To move an old qualified retirement account to a new retirement account or to a rollover IRA, you'll need to contact your previous employer's human resources department or the retirement plan administrator. They will have you complete a form that specifies which account you are moving and the account number of the new qualified retirement plan. After the paperwork is submitted, your old retirement plan will send the account funds to your new retirement plan. Be patient, since this process will usually take several weeks. If you left a retirement account with an old employer and you are not sure if the account still exists, the first step is to contact the National Registry of Unclaimed Retirement Benefits at https://www.unclaimedretirementbenefits.com.

The main advantage to moving all retirement accounts into a single individual retirement account (IRA) is that investing options increase greatly. A study investigating the adequacy of investment choices in 401(k) plans (Elton et al., 2004) found that only 28.8 percent of surveyed 401(k) plans offered 10 or more investment choices. The study also concluded that "for 62 percent of the plans, the types of choices offered are inadequate and that over a 20-year period this makes a difference in terminal wealth of over 300 percent." Reviewing the top holdings held by the domestic and international 401(k) investment options, many are nearly identical. In addition, few plans offer access to alternative asset classes such as real estate or commodities. The key idea behind adding other asset classes to your portfolio is that the added diversification benefits smoothes out the volatility. Put simply, you'll have some assets *zig* while others *zag*.

■ Investing: Mutual Funds

Mutual funds are the most likely investment used by financial planners today. The mutual fund, which is what most people invest in within their 401(k) plans, is a professionally managed and diversified portfolio of individual stocks, bonds, and other assets such as real estate, commodities, and currencies. The main benefit to the individual investor is access to these managed portfolios in a single transaction. It is important to note that mutual funds are not savings accounts or certificates of deposit. They are not guaranteed against loss by any government agency.

The number of mutual funds ranges into the thousands, but most of them have very similar strategies. While too numerous to list here, the typical funds will invest in individual stocks (domestic and international), government and corporate bonds (domestic and international), real estate (domestic and international), commodities (domestic and international), and a wide array of alternative strategies. There are volumes dedicated solely to portfolio construction. The selection of the perfect mutual fund for your retirement assets is certainly a tricky subject, but the one point that can be made that will apply to every investor is the subject of mutual fund fees.

Mutual funds are like any other company. They have expenses associated with running the fund and compensation for managing the fund. These fees can be as low as 0.10 percent of fund assets to 3 percent or more for complex portfolio strategies. In 2007, the average fund expense was 0.90 percent (Morningstar.com). That means that for every $10,000 you've invested in a mutual fund, $90 will automatically go to the fund for expenses over the course of a year. When considering funds, everything else being equal, lower expenses are definitely better.

Another expense related to mutual funds is known as the 12b-1 fee, which is an annual marketing or distribution fee on a mutual fund. The 12b-1 fee is considered an operational expense and, as such, is included in a fund's expense ratio. It is generally between 0.25 and 1 percent (the maximum allowed) of a fund's net assets. The fee gets its name from a section in the Investment Company Act of 1940. Sometimes these fees are not included in a company's annual expense ratio and can add to the administrative costs of owning a mutual fund. You should verify the 12b-1 fee before investing in a fund. Most investment professionals believe that the mutual fund industry should have moved beyond charging 12b-1 fees and that their only purpose is to increase a fund's profits for the funds that still charge them.

Some mutual funds and brokers utilize sales "loads"—a fee or commission—on their funds. There are two main types of sales loads charged: the front-load and the back-end load. The most typical, and the one that concerns us most, is the front-load sales charge. Many brokers and their representatives still work on commission, which means their income is based on how much they sell you. Some brokers and their reps will charge up to an 8 percent sales commission. Many of the most common funds charge investors up to 5.75 percent to purchase a fund. That means for every $10,000 invested, the investor pays a $575 sales charge. Before the assets even reach the mutual fund to be invested, the investor is down 5.75 percent and requires a 6.1 percent gain to break even. Plus, the mutual funds still charge an annual expense fee to fund their business operations.

It is very important to understand that many mutual funds are available with no front- or back-load charges. No-load mutual funds can be purchased or sold for a flat fee ranging between $10 and $100 through online brokers. In some cases, mutual funds can be purchased or sold with no fees at all. Why do investors pay such large sales loads? Because, unfortunately, there are broker-dealers such as Edward Jones who, in 2004, were forced to pay fines of $75 million to their customers. Edward Jones had failed to tell its customers that they were promoting a certain mutual fund family because of a revenue sharing agreement and not because of the fund family's long-term investment objectives and performance (http://www.sec.gov/news/press/2004-177.htm).

During 2003 and 2004, the National Association of Securities Dealers (NASD) brought more than 80 enforcement actions for violations of the sale of mutual funds and pooled investment products. Violations in these cases included suitability of the mutual fund share classes that brokers recommended, sales practices, improper disclosures, and compensation arrangements between the funds and brokers. These actions bring to more than 200 the number of cases NASD has taken against mutual fund companies and securities sales people since 2000. In addition, and most recently, NASD has brought enforcement actions dealing with market timing and the improper failure of a broker-dealer to waive certain sales charges or to deliver promised discounts on front-end load sales charges (http://www.finra.org/Newsroom/Speeches/Schapiro/P011027).

In 2001, Morey studied the performance of mutual funds with and without sales loads. It was determined that before adjusting for sales loads, no-load funds performed slightly better. After adjusting for the sales load, no-load funds were found to perform much better than funds with sales loads. The study also found that there was no significant difference between load funds that charged a higher or lower load amount than the industry load-average (Morey, 2001). This is not to say that there aren't load funds that have significantly out-performed no-load funds in the same investment objective class, but the study referenced certainly suggests that any fund that charges a sales fee of 5 percent just to get in the door is not in your best interest.

■ Should You Manage Your Own Portfolio?

Have you ever managed your own portfolio in the past? Are you good at developing and sticking to a plan? Can you ignore the investment pundits? Do you know the difference between a stock, mutual fund, and exchange-traded fund? Unless you can answer yes to these questions, you should not risk managing your retirement portfolio. Managing your retirement assets is not a hobby, or something you do when you feel like it; your retirement assets will be your main source of income for 20 or 30 years, or more, and should be viewed and managed with all the seriousness it deserves.

For those retirees who couldn't answer "yes" to all the questions, but want to try managing their resources themselves, we suggest that you manage no more than 2 or 3 percent of your total investments and allow a professional to manage the remainder. If you can prove to yourself that you can manage your own portfolio, then take on the remaining assets. If, however, you manage to lose half of the 2 or 3 percent you manage, it still only represents a small portion of your total assets and is not a major blow to your retirement plan.

With a little extra work, there is no reason why an individual or retired couple can't plan their own retirement, select investments, and manage their portfolios. However, for those who don't want the challenge or feel that they need some guidance, there are many options.

▣ References

Elton, Edwin, Martin Gruber, and Christopher Blake. 2004. "The Adequacy of Investment Choices Offered By 401(k) Plans."

Morey, Matthew R., 2001. "Should You Carry the Load? A Comprehensive Analysis of Load and No-Load Mutual Fund Out-of-Sample Performance." Dept. of Finance, Lubin School of Business, Pace University, New York, NY.

U.S. Bureau of Labor Statistics. 2008. TED: Youngest Boomers: 10.8 Jobs from Ages 18–42. http://www.bls.gov/opub/ted/2008/jun/wk5/art01.htm

11 ▪ ▪ ▪

Investing

What is investment risk? It could be defined as the risk of loss or loss beyond a certain percent, or it could be the risk of not meeting a specified goal or long-term obligations. Typically most investors, money managers, and advisors define investment risk as the variation of returns versus an expected long-term average return. Specifically, investment risk is defined by most as the standard deviation of returns, or the range of returns one would expect to achieve 67 percent of the time. Since 1972, the Standard & Poor's (S&P) 500 stock index has had an annual return of 11.2 percent and a standard deviation of 17.0 percent. While a definition of standard deviation is beyond the scope of this book, it is typically used as a measure of "risk" or "volatility" of an investment or portfolio of investments. The risk is presented as the variation of potential returns or how "noisy" the annual returns will be compared with the average annual return. Therefore, if the average annual return of the S&P 500 index is 11.2 percent and the standard deviation (risk) is 17 percent, one would expect a range of returns for the S&P 500 Index between −5.8 percent and 28.2 percent approximately 67 percent of the time. Clearly, given equal expected returns, smaller risk is preferable. The question then, is how does one achieve a lower-risk investment portfolio and still achieve some level of growth to meet future retirement income obligations?

▨ Bonds as Risk Reduction?

Outside of cash to cover living expenses for the next several months or years, bonds (government and corporate) have a place in every investment portfolio. A long-standing rule-of-thumb is that the percentage of bonds that should make a portfolio is simply equal to the investor's age. For example, a 50-year-old would allocate 50 percent of his or her portfolio to stocks and 50 percent to bonds. A 65-year-old investor would allocate 35 percent to stocks and 65 percent to bonds.

What is this bond allocation supposed to do for the portfolio? As of late 2008, the yield on a 10-year U.S. Treasury Note was yielding near 2.5 percent. If inflation remains near the longer-term averages of 3–4 percent, and especially if bonds are held in a taxable account, the real return on those bonds is near zero and at times could be negative. Furthermore, bonds are often included in portfolios as *risk reducers*. Bonds are included to mute the big swings in the stock market, insulating the investor from major market downswings. How effective are bonds at accomplishing this task? According to a study by Edward Qian of PanAgora, bonds act as a poor risk reducer to a fully invested portfolio until the bond allocation reaches 77 percent of the portfolio (Qian, 2005). Below a 77 percent bond allocation, large swings in stock prices simply outweigh the "stability" of bonds. The bear market and credit crisis in 2008 confirms this. The following table outlines returns from the market peak on October 2007 through October 2008. Included in the table is the 60/40 stock-and-bond portfolio that is so often utilized by investors and their brokers to create a "conservative" allocation portfolio.

In the case of the 2008 bear market, the conservative allocation portfolio did not substantially reduce risk and has left the conservative investor with significant losses. It wasn't until the bond allocation exceeded 75 percent of the portfolio that the bonds actually had a marked effect on risk reduction. Furthermore, when markets do recover, the small allocation of stocks significantly limits the growth potential of the portfolio that is heavily weighted towards bonds.

▨ Reducing Investment Portfolio Risk

Modern Portfolio Theory

In 1990, Harry Markowich published his work on Modern Portfolio Theory. In essence, it was shown that there indeed is a free lunch when it comes to

Table 11.1
Stock Market Returns, 2007–2008

	Wilshire 5000 total stock market index (VTSMX)	Vanguard total bond Fund (VMBFX)	60% Stocks 40% bonds	23% Stocks 77% Bonds
10/9/07	$37.09	$9.49		
10/27/08	$20.36	$9.66		
Total Return	−45.11%	1.79%	−26.35%	−9.00%

(source: finance.yahoo.com)

investing: asset allocation. By allocating an investment portfolio across multiple asset classes with low correlation, investment return increases for a given level of risk, where risk is measured as the volatility of returns.

Asset classes could include, but certainly aren't limited to: U.S. stocks, international stocks, emerging market stocks, U.S. treasury bonds, corporate bonds, real estate, commodities, and a multitude of subsets of those broad asset classes.

The following chart shows the relationship between risk and reward for a portfolio of U.S. stocks and bonds. The data points, beginning at the bottom left, are 100 percent bonds with each date point increasing U.S. stock allocation by 5 percent. At the top right, the last data point represents a portfolio of 100 percent U.S. stocks.

As one would expect, the portfolio returns increase with each additional increase in stocks, with a corresponding increase in portfolio volatility.

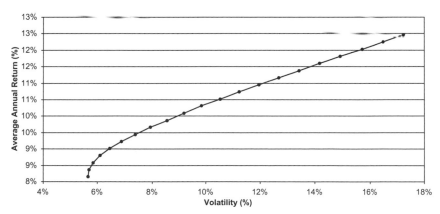

Figure 11.1
Risk and Reward: U.S. Stocks and Bonds

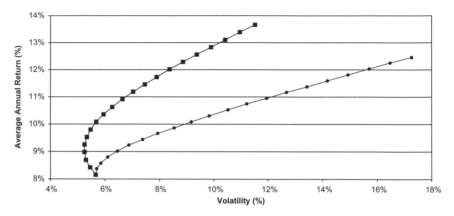

Figure 11.2
Risk vs. Reward: Five Asset Classes

If we apply Modern Portfolio Theory and include asset classes beyond U.S. stocks, such as international stocks, real estate, and commodities, all in equal amounts, the risk-return curve begins to look a little different, as shown in the following chart.

By diversifying the non-bond assets into several asset classes, the risk-reward curve changes dramatically. By splitting the U.S. stock allocation equally between U.S. stocks, international stocks, real estate, and commodities, one can both reduce risk *and* increase portfolio returns. (Data source: http://www.assetplay.net/financial-tools/risk-reward.html, returns based on 1972–2007 data.)

The most notable investors utilizing the Modern Portfolio Theory principles are several university endowments, including Harvard and Yale. David Swensen, investment manager for the Yale endowment, has written two books on the subject and has been interviewed by both the *New York Times* and on National Public Radio, discussing how the individual investor can implement the endowment-like portfolio. However, in a September 2007 *Pensions & Investments* interview, Harvard's Mohamed El-Erian, then the president of the Harvard Management Co., said in response to the suggestion that the benefits of diversification have been getting diluted, that:

"It's getting very crowded, not only in terms of asset allocations, but in terms of finding the right implementation vehicles. There's a limit to how much superior investment expertise is out there. So the asset allocation is going to be less potent because there are more people doing it. And then the global liquidity situation is changing as well. So our view is that performance in future needs something more—two things more: first, better risk management, because correlated risk has become a big issue, and diversified asset allocation no longer gives you the risk mitigating characteristics it used to. Second, is identifying new secular themes that will play out over the next five years, and trying to be a first mover in those, and that's what we're working very hard at doing" (Appell, 2007).

It's unlikely that an individual investor or even most professional investment managers will be able to compete with the Harvard or Yale investment selection for new secular themes, but it would be important to note the first point, which is that better risk management is necessary as diversified asset allocation no longer is providing the benefits it once did. ("Secular themes" means finding new and different investment opportunities or those that are not necessarily related to the U.S. stock or bond markets.

Better Risk Reduction

The cornerstone of Modern Portfolio Theory is that uncorrelated assets, when combined in a diversified portfolio, will increase investment returns for a given level of risk in comparison with a nondiversified portfolio with the same level of risk. But what happens when the majority of asset classes become highly correlated? That is, what happens when the majority of stocks and other assets all go down in price at the same time?

Proactive risk management is not intended to "beat the market," but instead to achieve market-like returns with much less volatility. This is usually achieved by reducing or eliminating market exposure at critical points; attempting to gain from the majority of asset class advances (months and years); and attempting to avoid the majority of asset class declines.

Stock-market-like return with lower volatility has several key advantages. First, is compounded annual growth rate, or CAGR. Given the following annual returns from two separate investments, which would you rather have, Investment A or B?

Investment A	Investment B
7%	15%
6%	20%
8%	21%
5%	−15%
7%	−8%

Many investors would pick Investment B, despite the two negative years, because they were less than the positive years. However, both investments have the same average return over five years of 6.60 percent. Moreover, when one compounds those returns:

$$\text{Investment A} = (1+.07) \times (1+.06) \times (1+.08) \times (1+.05) \times (1+.07) - 1 \times 100\%$$

Investment A = 37.622% Total Return or 6.595% CAGR
   and,
Investment B = $(1+.15) \times (1+.20) \times (1+.21) \times (1-.15) \times (1-.08) - 1 \times$
   100%
Investment B = 30.578% Total Return or 5.481% CAGR

Note that the volatility of returns, which is actually the standard deviation of returns, is 1.14 percent and 16.86 percent for Investments A and B, respectively. By reducing the variation between annual returns, even though those returns are much less dramatic, Investment A actually grew more (7.044 percent more!) than Investment B over five years.

This example was designed to make a point. However, there is a second advantage to low volatility that is equally important—sticking with an investment strategy for the long term. Investors, while instructed to buy-and-hold for the long term, are most likely to sell at market bottoms when they can't sleep at night, and are most likely to buy back in after the market has rallied appreciably, after it has become "safe" again. By reducing the volatility in the investment strategy, investors are much more likely to remain vested in the strategy and not suffer the emotional swings that otherwise shake them out of what could be a sound strategy.

Several asset managers, including this author, have implemented active risk-reduction strategies to reduce volatility for their clients' portfolios using a combination of trend-following and market-timing strategies. Merriman and Tilley of the Merriman Capital Group (Merriman, 1999–2002) and Mebane Faber (Faber, 2007) have presented several sources and strategy tests on simple asset-market timing systems that have been effective in reducing portfolio risk. Note that none of the strategies' attempts to beat the market are used simply to sidestep the wealth-erasing bear markets that occur in every asset class. These strategies have proven most effective in 2008 as many asset classes are down by 40 to 50 percent; a simple timing strategy reduced those losses to the low single digits.

Following is the same chart as shown previously, but with the single data point added. That data point is the average annual return and volatility from an equal weighted portfolio of U.S. stocks, international stocks, real estate, commodities, and bonds (20 percent in each asset), with a simple risk-management timing system proposed by Faber (2007).

Why is risk reduction so important? Consider the 26 percent loss in the 60/40 portfolio in a previous table. That portfolio must now grow by more than 35 percent just to reach previous levels. If an investor is also withdrawing income from the portfolio, it will require further growth. Those investors who held stocks throughout the entire 2008 market decline will require their portfolios to double in value to reach breakeven. Those investors who moved their assets to cash or bonds as we entered the bear market and are down 10 percent, will only require an 11.1 percent move in their portfolio to reach previous peak levels. Following are some things you need

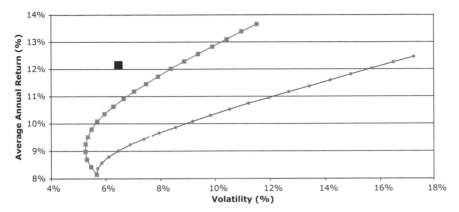

Figure 11.3
Risk vs Reward: Simple Risk Management

to know if you are to become an astute investor or seek help from investment professionals.

Financial Planners

If you feel that you need help determining what you need for retirement assets and the best way to generate income from those assets, a good place to start is with a financial planner. The best way to find a financial planner is to ask friends and colleagues who they use. Most financial planners can help people with a wide range of retirement planning needs, including investments, insurance, estate planning, and taxes.

There are several professional designations for financial planners. The most common one is the certified financial planner (CFP). This designation requires extensive study, passing a comprehensive exam, work experience, continued education, and adherence to the CFP Board's Code of Ethics and Professional Responsibility. The CFP Web site (www.cfp.com) offers a search function to locate CFP practitioners.

Fiduciary Duties

The Investment Advisors Act of 1940 imposes a fiduciary duty on investment advisors. Specifically, fiduciary duty is a legal relationship of confidence or trust between two or more parties.

The general purpose of an investment advisor's fiduciary duty is to eliminate conflicts of interest and prevent an advisor from taking unfair advantage of a client's trust. In order to fulfill this duty, an investment advisor is required to always act in his or her clients' best interests, and to make full and fair disclosure of all material facts, especially when the advisor's interests may conflict with those of his clients (Giachetti, 2006).

Many financial professionals refer to themselves as "advisors" or "consultants," but who really has a fiduciary duty?

Type of Professional	Who is a Fiduciary?
Physician	Yes, follows Hippocratic oath
Lawyer	Yes
Stock Broker	No
Insurance Agent	No
Registered Representative	No
CFP Practitioner	Maybe*
Financial Planner	Maybe*
Registered Investment Advisor	Yes

(Source: www.focusonfiduciary.com)
*Note: In 2007, the CFP Board of Standards added to its code of ethics the principle of fiduciary duty to the client by all holders of the CFP certificates. However, it is still unclear if this has any legal standing beyond being denied the use of the CFP designation. Unless a CFP or financial planner is associated directly with someone who is designated as a Registered Investment Advisor, they are not necessarily a fiduciary.

The following is a broker-dealer disclosure as required by the Securities and Exchange Commission:

> Your account is a brokerage account and not an advisory account. Our interests may not always be the same as yours. Please ask us questions to make sure you understand your rights and our obligations to you, including the extent of our obligations to disclose conflicts of interest and to act in your best interest. We are paid both by you and, sometimes, by people who compensate us based on what you buy. Therefore, our profits, and our salespersons' compensation, may vary by product and over time. (Source: www.focusonfiduciary.com)

Does this imply that any financial consultant who is not a fiduciary will take advantage of a client? No, but it should be clear that any financial relationship should be based primarily on trust. When seeking advice and services, you should be clear about all fees charged, as well as the reasoning behind decisions made with your investment money. If the professional being consulted refuses or doesn't immediately tell you how they are being compensated, our suggestion is to thank them for their time and to look elsewhere for help.

■ References

Appell, Douglas. "Making the Grade: Face to Face with Harvard's Mohamed El-Erian." Pionline.com, September 3, 2007, http://www.pionline.com/apps/pbcs.dll/article?AID=/20070903/FACETOFACE/70831007/1039/PRINTSUB.

Faber, Mebane. Spring 2007. "A Quantitative Approach to Tactical Asset Allocation." *The Journal of Wealth Management.*

Giachetti, Thomas D. November 2006. "Defining fiduciary: What is an advisor's true fiduciary duty?" *Investment Advisor.*

Merriman, 1999–2002. All of the below can be found at www.fundadvice.com:

Tilley, Dennis. 1999. "Which is Better, Buy-and-hold or Market Timing?"

Tilley, Dennis. 1999. "Designing a Market Timing System to Maximize the Probability It Will Work."

Merriman, Paul. 2001. "All About Market Timing."

Merriman, Paul. 2001. "The Best Retirement Portfolio We Know."

Merriman, Paul. 2002. "The Best Retirement Strategy I Know Using Active Risk Management."

Merriman, Paul. 2002. "Market Timing's Bad Rap."

Morey, Matthew R. 2001. *Should You Carry the Load? A Comprehensive Analysis of Load and No-load Mutual Fund Out-of-Sample Performance.* Department of Finance, Lubin School of Business, Pace University, New York.

Qian, Edward. 2005. Risk Parity Portfolios: Efficient Portfolios Through True Diversification. PanAgora Asset Management. https://content.putnam.com/panagora/pdf/risk_party_portfolios.pdf.

U.S. Bureau of Labor Statistics. "Economic News Release: Number of Jobs Held, Labor Market Activity, and Earnings Growth among the Youngest Baby Boomers: Results from a Longitudinal Survey Summary (June 27, 2008), http://www.bls.gov/news.release/nlsoy.nr0.htm.

12 ■ ■ ■

Insurance and Estate Planning

■ Insurance

There are multiple types of insurance and many more ways to utilize insurance products in retirement planning and estate planning. Many retirees will find them useful; an equal number may find no need for additional insurance beyond that for health care, cars, and their home. The main types of insurance that you may find useful include life insurance, long-term care insurance, additional liability insurance, and a relatively new product, longevity insurance.

The primary purpose of insurance is to protect against the risk of a possible future loss. Life insurance will provide a benefit to the designated beneficiaries of the insurance contract in the event of the death of the policyholder. Long-term care insurance will provide for the extensive costs associated with prolonged assisted or nursing home care not covered by other health insurance, including Medicare or Medicaid. Liability insurance can provide for additional levels of coverage that protect retirement savings that may be more than the basic coverage provided by most auto and home coverage. Longevity insurance will pay out to retirees beyond a certain age to protect against the possibility of outliving other retirement income sources.

Insurance, like the rest of financial planning, is different for every circumstance. The following is meant to be an introduction to the basic types of insurance and how they are often utilized with the total financial planning framework; it is not meant to be a recommendation for any specific type. All types of insurance should be investigated further for financial planning use with the help of a financial planner and an insurance specialist. One common complaint surrounding the insurance industry is the complex commission and compensation structure, as well as the possibility that you'll be sold unsuitable insurance products. The best protection against this is to become an informed consumer and get multiple evaluations of your insurance needs. The insurance industry is regulated at the state level, and each state has a Web site dedicated to providing consumers with resources to look up insurance brokers and see if any complaints have been filed against them. An excellent resource for learning about insurance types is AARP.org.

Temporary (Term) Life Insurance

Term life insurance is a lot like insurance for your car—it provides coverage for a specified number of years for a specified premium. The policy does not accumulate cash value, but only buys time-limited protection should you die. There are generally three key factors to consider when buying term insurance: (a) the face amount (protection or death benefit); (b) the premium to be paid (cost to the insured); and (c) the length of coverage (term).

Insurance companies sell term insurance with many different combinations of the three key parameters. The face amount can remain constant or decline. The term can be for one or more years. The premium can remain level or increase. A common type of term insurance is called annual renewable term insurance. It is a one-year policy, but the insurance company guarantees it will issue the policy without regard to the insurability of the insured and with a premium set for the insured's age at that time. Another common type of term insurance is mortgage insurance, which has a level premium but declines each year in the value of the policy as the mortgage is paid off. The face amount is intended to equal the amount of the mortgage on the policy owner's residence so the mortgage will be paid if the insured dies.

Generally, term life insurance makes sense for younger families who want to ensure against the loss of one or both spouses. The insurance face value would need to be at least equivalent to a spouse's expected earnings needed to cover such expenses as the costs of raising a child and their college tuition, remaining mortgage principal debt, and the replacement of any anticipated retirement savings. Term life may also make sense for younger retirees who rely heavily on one spouse's defined benefit pension plan that lacks survivor benefits. An early death of the pension owner could jeopardize the retirement of the survivor. In this case, a term insurance policy could provide some level of protection. Note that most insurance companies limit their term policies to those less than 75 or so. It is also important to note that just like car insurance, if the insurance term is up, and the policyholder is still living, all of the premiums paid are not recoverable. To avoid losing an accumulation of premiums, you'd have to move on to a permanent or whole life insurance policy, discussed in the next section.

Premiums for term life insurance are affected by the age at which you purchase the policy. For example, the yearly premium for a 20-year-$500,000 term life insurance policy purchased by a 47–year-old male who hasn't smoked in three years and whose health is average would be $1,410 a year for 20 years or $28,200 over 20 years. The same policy purchased at 65 by a nonsmoking male whose health is average would cost $8,000 a year or $160,000 over 20 years. You can see that the insurance company believes that a man at 47 has eight times less risk of dying before the term of the policy ends than a man of 65 (Term Life Insurance Costs, 2008).

SmartMoney confirms that premiums for term insurance are fairly inexpensive for people in good health up to about age 50. After that age, as our example shows, premiums start to get progressively more expensive. According to *SmartMoney*, most companies simply won't sell term policies to people over age 65 (*SmartMoney Magazine*, 2008).

Permanent Life Insurance

Permanent life insurance remains in force until the policy matures (usually on the death of the insured) unless the owner fails to pay the premium when due. The policy cannot be canceled by the insurer for any reason except fraud in the application, and that cancellation must occur within a period of time defined by law (usually two years). Permanent insurance builds a cash value that reduces the amount at risk to the insurance company over time. This means that a policy with a million-dollar face value can be relatively expensive to a 70-year-old. The owner can access the money in the cash value by withdrawing money, borrowing the cash value, or surrendering the policy and receiving the surrender value.

There are three basic types of permanent insurance: whole life, universal life, and endowment. Instead of discussing the intricacies of each type, a discussion of whole life will help in understanding the concept.

Whole Life Coverage

Whole life insurance provides for a level premium and a cash value included in the policy guaranteed by the company. The primary advantages of whole life coverage are guaranteed death benefits, guaranteed cash values, and fixed and known annual premiums. The primary disadvantages of whole life are premium inflexibility and that the rate of return in the policy may not be competitive with other savings alternatives. Riders are available that can allow one to increase the death benefit by paying an additional premium. Premiums are much higher than term insurance in the short-term, but cumulative premiums are roughly equal if policies are kept in force until average life expectancy.

Cash value of the policy can be accessed at any time through policy "loans." Since these loans decrease the death benefit if not paid back, payback is optional. Cash values are not paid to the beneficiary upon the death of the insured; the beneficiary only receives the death benefit indicated in the policy. It is possible to buy additional death benefits through additions to the premiums paid.

There are some cases in which a whole life policy is sold as a "saving" or retirement investment because it accumulates a cash value. While it is true that the policy accumulates a cash value, the rate of return is generally quite a bit lower than true retirement savings and investments made through a 401(k) or individual retirement account. If retirement savings are needed, invest your assets where they can grow at a reasonable rate of return. If life insurance is needed, buy insurance. According to State Farm Insurance (2008), there are several benefits to whole life coverage:

1. In most cases, whole life insurance premiums are level, and, therefore, the younger you are when purchasing whole life, the cheaper the premiums will be.
2. Whole life insurance policies often earn dividends. If those dividends earned are greater than the policy cost, some of the insurance premium may be returned to the policy holder.
3. Whole life insurance policies, unlike term life, accumulate a cash value. Over time and after some amount of the premiums have been paid, there is a guaranteed payout if you decide to cancel the policy. In addition, one can also borrow against the accumulated cash value of the whole life policy.

The liabilities of whole life insurance, as noted by *SmartMoney* are that whole life insurance is expensive, and there are better ways of preparing for retirement. They write, "these policies come with high fees and commissions, which sometimes lop off as much as three percentage points from the annual return. On top of that, there are up-front (but hidden) commissions that are typically 100% of your first year's premium. Worse, it's often impossible to tell what the return on the investment will be, and how much of what you pay in goes toward the insurance and how much toward the investment" (*SmartMoney Magazine*, 2008).

There are additional permanent life insurance options, including universal life, equity-indexed universal life, and variable universal life, and all become increasingly complex. We suggest that anyone considering life insurance discuss it with a qualified financial planner or an independent insurance specialist. One should plan on asking lots of questions to understand what is being bought. Also, discuss how the financial professional is being compensated for selling a specific type of insurance product.

The cost of whole life insurance is much higher than term insurance because the policy is in effect until death. State Farm Insurance (2008) indicates that the same 47-year-old man we used as an example for term life insurance purchasing a whole life policy in force until death would pay a premium of $12,100 a year. A 65-year-old man would pay $31,980 a year for a whole life policy. At age 67, our 47-year-old man purchasing a guaranteed whole life policy would have death benefits of $500,000 plus a guaranteed cash value of $185,515. The cash value includes the dividends and interest that have accrued on the policy. At age 85, the same man would have a guaranteed cash value of $369,000. If he died at 85 and had not borrowed or taken out any of his dividends, his beneficiary would receive his guaranteed death benefit of $500,000 plus his guaranteed cash value of $369,000, for a total death benefit to his beneficiary of $869,000. By multiplying his premium of $12,100 by 38 years, at age 85 he would have paid the insurance company $456,000 in premiums to make $869,000. Obviously, he would have made much more by investing in a mutual fund and even by purchasing high-yield CDs. The benefit of the guaranteed whole life policy is that should he die young, his beneficiary would have a substantial death benefit.

▦ Caution

Before you buy an insurance policy, make sure to check out the company. According to *SmartMoney* (2008), information on the credit worthiness of insurance companies is easy to obtain. While you can always contact the insurance company directly and ask about its ratings, it's best to get this information independently. *SmartMoney* recommends that you only select insurance companies rated A or better; the most financially sound insurers are rated AAA.

An excellent Web site in terms of detail and ease of use (and it's free) is insure.com, where you can get ratings online, as well as comprehensive reports on individual insurers. Duff & Phelps ratings of claims-paying ability are available free at dcrco.com. AM Best (ambest.com) is also an excellent resource, although a report will cost $35. Make sure any report you get is from within the last six months, and be careful not to use dated reports. In the current economic climate, things change quickly, and a year-old report may give you useless information.

▪ Long-term Care Insurance

You may never need long-term care. But in 2008, about 9 million men and women over the age of 65 needed it. By 2020, 12 million older Americans will need long-term care. Most will be cared for at home; family and friends are the sole caregivers for 70 percent of the elderly. A study by the U.S. Department of Health and Human Services says that people who reach age 65 will likely have a 40 percent chance of entering a nursing home. About 10 percent of the people who enter a nursing home will stay there five years or more (HHS[a], 2008).

Long-term care insurance generally covers home care, assisted living, adult day care, and nursing home care. Essentially, any type of care can be purchased. It can pay for a visiting or live-in caregiver, housekeeper, or 24/7 private duty nurse (up to the policy benefit maximum).

According to the U.S. Department for Health and Human Services National Clearinghouse for Long-term Care Information, the average costs for care in the United States (HHS[b], 2008) are:

- $187/day for a semiprivate room in a nursing home
- $209/day for a private room in a nursing home
- $3,008/month for care in an assisted living facility (for a one-bedroom unit)
- $29/hour for a home health aide
- $18/hour for homemaker services
- $59/day for care in an adult day health care center.

A single year's stay in a private room nursing home would cost $76,285 using the average cost of $209 per day. The average annual cost of long-term care insurance for all age groups is only $1,973 per year (HHS, 2005). The annual cost of long-term care insurance is definitely a bargain compared to the annual cost of the average nursing home facility. Like most insurance, long-term care insurance can be highly customized to meet the needs of the insured. Like whole life insurance, long-term care insurance is generally less expensive when purchased at a younger age.

Medicaid does provide some amount of the benefits of long-term care insurance. It provides medically necessary services for people with limited resources who need nursing home care but can stay at home with special community care services (CMS, 2008). However, Medicaid generally does not cover long-term care provided in a home setting or for assisted living. People who need long-term care often prefer care in the home or in a private room in an assisted living facility.

Generally, Medicare doesn't pay for long-term care; it pays only for medically necessary skilled nursing facility or home health care. However, you must meet certain conditions for Medicare to pay for these types of care.

Most long-term care is to assist people with support services such as activities of daily living like dressing, bathing, and using the bathroom. Medicare doesn't pay for this type of care, called "custodial care." Custodial care (non-skilled care) is care that helps you with activities of daily living. It may also include care that most people do for themselves, for example, diabetes monitoring. Some Medicare Advantage Plans (formerly Medicare + Choice) may offer limited skilled nursing facility and home care (skilled care) coverage if the care is medically necessary. You may have to pay some of the costs.

Longevity Insurance

Longevity insurance is a relatively new insurance product and is designed to protect the retiree from outliving their assets by providing some predetermined amount of income at a specified age. The insurance is typically purchased at the time of retirement. There are several points to consider: first, if the beneficiary dies before the specified age, the insurance company keeps all the premiums paid; second, it is important to consider the effects of inflation on the amount of income purchased. That is, $100 of income today will not buy the same amount of goods and services in 20 years. Purchase the amount of income you'll need in 20 years, not the amount you need at the time of purchase.

A Business Wire press release regarding Metlife's "Longevity Insurance" offering wrote: "For example, an employee age 55 may decide that he or she wants income payments to start at age 85. If that employee had purchased Retirement Income Insurance today with a single sum purchase amount of $25,000, starting at age 85 he or she could expect to receive $22,000 annually, which would be guaranteed for the rest of that person's life. Payments begin when other funds may be running low and are guaranteed to last for the rest of the individual's life" (BW, 2004). What this example fails to state is that after 30 years of 3 percent inflation, that $22,000 will only purchase the equivalent of $9,063.

Estate Planning

Note to reader: Neither author is an expert in estate planning. The following is provided as an overview for the benefit of educating the reader. We encourage every reader to review their will and estate plan with a qualified attorney who specializes in estate planning and is familiar with state laws regulating estates. Many estate-planning attorneys will offer a set-price or low consultation fee to review your estate planning needs in the range of $200 to $300. In the majority of cases, this review will be more than adequate to ensure that your will or estate plan is sufficient.

If you own any assets, you have an estate. An estate encompasses anything of value to which the deceased person was or might have been entitled to claim during his or her lifetime. The property of the estate must either be distributed through a will or transferred through the laws of intestacy if there is no will. A will is the most commonly used legal instrument for the distribution of the property and is certainly the easiest to create. However, before property can be disposed of according to the terms of a will, the will must be submitted to a probate court having jurisdiction of the estate. Probate is often considered a relatively lengthy and expensive process, albeit one that may provide greater safeguards with regard to the rights of a deceased person's beneficiaries. Probate is, however, often contested by creditors or disgruntled members of the family of the deceased who feel they have not received their fair share of the deceased's property.

If the estate is relatively simple, with only one or two beneficiaries, it makes sense to establish a simple will. If, however, there are multiple beneficiaries, sometimes from more than one marriage plus multiple homes, it would be preferable to bypass the probate process altogether by creating a trust.

■ Trusts

In order to expedite the process of transferring assets to intended beneficiaries, it is beneficial to arrange property so it can bypass the probate process. For example, placing property into a trust before death will often allow the accomplishment of the objectives of property distribution without coming under the jurisdiction of a court and possible redistribution after a lengthy contested probate process and trial. Similarly, jointly held property (in common law systems), life insurance, annuities, qualified retirement plans (401(k)s, 403(b)s, etc.), or IRAs will also avoid probate as these devices allow property to transfer to beneficiaries outside the probate process.

Which is right for you? Unfortunately, for all but the simplest cases, the best thing to do is discuss estate planning with a financial planner or with an attorney who specializes in estate planning and all of laws surrounding it.

■ Estate Planning for Everyone

Everyone who has a retirement account at work, an IRA, annuities, or life insurance can accomplish a majority of the estate-planning process. Each retirement plan or insurance product allows for the designation of one or many separate beneficiaries. Make sure that these are up to date and represent current circumstances. If one were to die with the designated beneficiary of their IRA as an ex-spouse, legally, that IRA will be transferred to that person. If you're not sure how to make that change, contact the retirement plan administrator, the holder of the IRA, or the insurance company, and find out how to change it.

For assets that do not allow for designation of beneficiaries, like a savings or investment account, consider a transfer-on-death (TOD) designation for the account. This TOD also allows one to bypass probate and transfer the assets directly to the beneficiary. Again, this works very well in the simplest circumstances. With larger estates and multiple beneficiaries, other options such as living trusts could be more appropriate and should be discussed with a qualified financial planner or estate attorney.

▨ Useful Web Site

AARP. www.aarp.org.

▨ References

Business Wire. "MetLife Introduces 'Longevity Insurance' to Help Protect against Outliving Retirement Savings in Later Years." September 15, 2004, http://www.insurancenewsnet.com/article.asp?a=1&id=25039.

Centers for Medicare & Medicaid Services. 2008. http://www.cms.hhs.gov/MedicaidEligibility/02_AreYouEligible_.asp.

SmartMoney Magazine. 2008. "Term or Whole Insurance?" http://www.smartmoney.com/insurance/life/index.cfm?story=lifeterm.

State Farm Insurance. 2008. Whole Life Insurance. http://www.statefarm.com/insurance/life_annuity/life/whole/whole.asp.

Term Life Insurance Costs. 2008. Budget Life Insurance Quotes. https://www.budgetlife.com/expertquotes.htm.

U.S. Department of Health and Human Services. 2005. Long-Term Care Insurance Costs and Receiving Benefits. http://www.longtermcare.gov/LTC/Main_Site/Paying_LTC/Private_Programs/LTC_Insurance/index.aspx#LTCICRD.

U.S. Department of Health and Human Services. 2008. Long-Term Care. http://www.medicare.gov/LongTermCare/Static/Home.asp.

U.S. Department of Health and Human Services. 2008. What Does Long-Term Care Cost? http://www.longtermcare.gov/LTC/Main_Site/Paying_LTC/Costs_Of_Care/Costs_Of_Care.aspx#What.

Part III

THE RETIREMENT DECISION

Chapters 13 and 14 discuss the difficult task of deciding when you will retire and then following through with the decision. We strongly recommend the inclusion of loved ones in that decision, and discuss what happens in relationships when spouses and family are not consulted. Chapter 14 considers the stress involved in making the decision, why the decision is so stressful, and what you can do to reduce your stress.

13 ■ ■ ■

Involving Family Members in Retirement Decisions

Retirement affects everyone in a family. For that reason, you should talk over your plans with your extended family, including your friends. Many of them have stereotypes of retired living that are often not true, unrealistic, or don't apply to you. It's important that you deal with these misconceptions so you have a supportive family and a core of understanding friends to help you move toward and into retirement. Some issues that family members may wish to discuss openly with you include:

- Your children may be concerned that you may spend too much time with them.
- Your spouse may worry that with extra time on your hands you might demand a great deal of his or her time and attention.
- Concerns may exist over whether you will have enough money, and in the event of your death, how your estate will be dealt with and whether it will be apportioned fairly.
- Friends may see you as being very active and wonder if you'll be able to handle this extra leisure time.

These are all legitimate issues to consider and your response should be thoughtful, measured, and honest.

We sometimes believe that children and family members will let us down as we age, particularly when we are in need of physical and emotional assistance, but Glaser and colleagues (2008) found that to the contrary, children often help out when older adult marriages dissolve or in the event of the death of a spouse, which makes their input into the retirement decision vital. The researchers note that much of the current literature points to distancing by family members if a retired loved one divorces, but the researchers found a changing attitude toward the divorcing parent who remarries, and as much help given when needed to that parent as when that parent was still married to his or her long-term mate.

What we do know for certain is that some older adults have had troubled relationships with their children over a long period of time. This is particularly true of parents who were abusive, failed to form an attachment because of a lack of commitment to their children, and who abused alcohol and drugs. To think that these children will form positive attachments with their older adult parents and provide supportive help when it's needed may be unrealistic. Shu (2005) reports that almost two-thirds (67 percent) of all elder abuse is committed by adult children and their spouses. Before plans are made to heavily involve yourself with adult children and their families, you need to evaluate the quality of your relationship with your adult children and determine whether they will help out when you are in need. This is an important topic that you should discuss with your children before retirement. If they seem ambivalent about helping, you'll need to consider other options in case a health-related, emotional, or financial crisis occurs.

Nuttman-Schwartz (2007) notes the importance of involving family members in early retirement planning. The researcher writes, "The results [of his study] showed family perceptions' contribute to postretirement adjustment. Thus, in order to help the retirees to accept their retirement transition, it suggests that the pre-retirement intervention should focus on the family as a whole, especially when retirees plan their future" (p. 192). According to the author, pre-planning with family is particularly important when the retiree shows signs of loneliness and depression before retirement, since those emotional states may continue and even worsen after retirement.

Carpenter and colleagues (2006) found that adult children sometimes know their parents' preferences for retired life but are often unaware of many important issues, particularly those that pertain to achieving a high quality of life. The researchers suggest that families engage themselves in discussions of late-life issues and find out parental preferences. The authors recognize that families may not have these discussions "because of time constraints, discomfort bringing up topics that imply eventual impairment, or simply because families lack the tools to have productive discussions about preferences" (p. 562). The authors suggest a family process to reevaluate and accommodate the changing needs and preferences of older adults as they consider and move into retirement. The researchers conclude by saying that "[b]ecause most children inevitably play some role in guiding the psychosocial care of their parents, it is imperative to find ways to improve their knowledge about parent preferences and values" (p. 562).

▓ Advice for Family Members

The first thing you should recognize is that the entire notion of retirement is anxiety provoking for many retirees, primarily because it may suggest that productive life is over and that a gradual decline in health and life satisfaction is about to occur. It may also initiate fears about financial instability and boredom. So don't be surprised if your loved ones have fears and unrealistic expectations, or they just don't want to talk about retirement. All these reactions are common and are increasingly important to discuss as the person moves closer to making the decision to retire. Your support can be very helpful. Calm listening and trying to understand the retiree's concerns is the best antidote to pre-retirement anxiety. Attacking ideas or perceptions or saying that you've read negative things about the decisions a loved one is considering is never a good way to show that you care or that you want to help. There is no better way to find out about retirement than reading good research-oriented articles and talking to older adults you respect who have gone through what your loved one is going through.

Early retirement is a particularly difficult decision to make since it often comes when older adults are burned out on work or have enough money saved so work isn't really necessary. Most of the research suggests that people who retire early have issues related to boredom and are less satisfied than their later-retiring counterparts. This isn't always the case, but it's something to think about. What the early retiree might need is a break from work to get over stress and to get his or her creative juices flowing again. The best advice to loved ones considering early retirement is to tell them to keep their options open.

We recently spoke to a 62-year-old man we'd met at an out-of-town tennis tournament, and who had retired recently. Clearly, he was burned out over the increasingly stressful job of trying to keep a health care organization afloat while hearing constant complaints from patients, doctors, employees, and insurance companies. He told us he had no desire to work again and said that he was fully occupied with hiking, mountain bike riding, and seeing his grandchildren. He kept chatting long after we were finished playing tennis, and one had the feeling that as burned out as he no doubt was, he had a lot more work left in him. We suggested that he keep his options open just in case he needed something to do at some point. He mulled it over and said that he had many options if he got bored and that maybe he'd pursue them. We thought that was a wise decision. You don't go from running a multimillion-dollar hospital to taking care of grandkids overnight without some potential for boredom.

We wondered how his children felt about his plan to see them more frequently. He said they were happy about it, hesitated, and then said he *assumed* they were happy about it, but hadn't discussed it in any depth with them. We thought it would be a good idea if he did. He told us a week later that while his kids sounded happy about his plan to visit often, there was a subtle suggestion that it ought not be *too* often or *too* long. He was surprised and a little hurt, but guessed it was better to find out now rather than later, and then he went on to discuss a part-time work possibility he had, and how he thought maybe a couple of months of doing nothing might get him back in the mood to work again, but nothing, he added, as stressful as his work as a hospital administrator. He said, "The American health care system is tilting toward being broken and trying to keep things together is a job I never want to tackle again." He also admitted that he was divorced and a bit lonely, and that maybe finding a mate was what he should do instead of spending too much times with his grandkids. He asked if we knew any eligible single women in town. Yes, we said, we did, and that we'd chat with them first, and if they wanted to follow up, we'd give them his name and he or they could call. Amazing what people tell you at the tennis courts.

Why would such a high-level person have such a limited retirement plan? Not having a spouse or mate to discuss his plan with is certainly one reason. When you're single you get used to making your own decisions without consulting others. Burnout drove his retirement decision, and that's never a good motivator to retire because often when we leave the situation causing our burnout, our energy and drive return, and then what? Finally, he needed to chat about his plans in a quiet and ongoing way with his kids. He admitted that most of the talking he'd done about retirement was initiated during family reunions when people were happy and a little drunk, and that it was no place or time to talk about serious matters. We agreed.

We would also suggest that family members attend pre-retirement seminars with you. Being able to talk about the material in the seminars with family members helps process how you will approach a number of retirement issues. Even though you may not be ready to retire, attending pre-retirement seminars a year or two before you intend to retire gives you time to consider and plan for the many issues that retirement presents, such as where to live, whether you want to continue working, financial stability, spending more time with your children, understanding Social Security, other pensions, and Medicare, and having your health fully evaluated and any medical issues dealt with.

Hershey and colleagues (2003) found that pre-retirement seminars focusing on financial issues related to retirement had a positive impact on financial planning, but that carryover of learning often required a family member or friend to be present to reinforce what had been covered in the seminar for it to have a lasting impact. The authors write, "Clearly, one of the more prominent take-away messages from this investigation is that a relatively brief financial information intervention can have a positive effect on retirement planning, goal-setting, and savings practices" (p. 555).

Discussing the complex issues that affect married couples when one spouse is considering retirement, Pienta (2003) writes, "As more married couples enter their pre-retirement years, complex work and family issues will rise to the surface" (p. 355). Some of those issues include age differences in working couples in which the wife (or husband) has more years to work before retirement than the retiring spouse and how that affects retirement plans and retirement satisfaction. Another issue is that the younger working spouse will probably bring in more money than the retired spouse. Will this create problems in the relationship? Large age differences in spouses sometimes mean that the younger spouse may become a caretaker of the older spouse while they are still working, upsetting the younger spouse's retirement plans. Being together much of the time after retirement sometimes creates its own set of problems. Issues relating to money and inheritances may create considerable family antagonism. For these reasons, Pienta suggests the use of retirement counselors to help with future and ongoing issues related to retirement. Even though few people utilize retirement counselors at present (Turner, Bailey, and Scott, 1994), we think it's a very good idea in that specially trained retirement counselors can resolve problems that are difficult to anticipate, but which seriously affect the couple.

▓ A Case Example of Family Involvement in a Retirement Issue

Jane (62) and Sam (72) own a real estate agency in the Southwest. Sam has had multiple health problems over the past few years, but has done well enough to function on his own without much help from Jane. Lately, however, Sam has begun to deteriorate physically—he experiences ongoing angina attacks and difficulties in breathing that require Jane to spend a great deal of time transporting him to various doctors and hospitals, some at a distance from their home. As a consequence, their business is suffering and the commissions they should be earning are going to other agents. This financial setback has delayed Jane's retirement plans and created animosities in the marriage where none existed before. Sam and Jane have three adult children who decided to call a family meeting and have an intervention of sorts. Sam realizes that Jane is upset with her caretaking duties, and he feels awful that Jane's retirement plans are on hold while she spends much of her time caring for him. In a lengthy conversation over several weeks, the family decided on the following plan:

1. They will set aside one day a week for a designated family member to take Sam to his appointments, see the doctor with him, and make certain that he receives whatever medications or aftercare have been recommended.
2. In the event of an emergency, the family will have a designated family member take Sam for medical care.
3. If that family member is unavailable and no one else is available, they will contract with a local cab company to provide immediate transportation, and then a family member or Jane will come to the medical facility as soon as they are available.
4. Jane will be allowed to continue earning commissions and increase their financial stability so she can retire in three years.
5. After they retire, Sam and Jane would like to live on the beach in Mexico where they own a small condo. Because of Sam's medical problems and the uncertain availability of good medical care in Mexico, their son, a physician, will go with them to interview physicians in Mexico to see if competent emergency medical help would be available when needed.
6. The family will evaluate emergency medical plans to airlift Sam back to the United States for serious medical help if needed.
7. Once assured of good medical care, Sam and Jane plan to retire in three years, with Sam helping with the business to the extent that his health allows.

We spoke to Jane after the family intervention. She told us that the family discussions had helped resolve a situation that was creating a great deal of animosity in an otherwise loving couple. Jane said, "I guess it never dawned on me that Sam would ever need someone to take care of him. He's always been an independent and energetic man, and I guess it was sort of a shock to begin realizing he was also human and as open to illness as any of us. The family getting together and helping out made all the difference. Of course, we should have done this early on when Sam began to have heart problems but, like a lot of us who live busy lives, we didn't. I would tell anyone now, and I have told some of my friends, that having a plan before you run into an emergency is the best way to prevent the sort of bad feelings I was beginning to have toward taking care of Sam. I think he's relieved as well. Since we all conferred, Sam's been feeling better and helping much more with the business. I think it's taken a load off his mind as well."

▧ Summary

This chapter discusses the importance of involving loved ones in the retirement decision as well as your retirement plans. Several studies are reported showing that children and other family members can be very involved in retirement planning and can help with difficult retirement decisions. The chapter strongly advises that pre-retirement seminars should be attended with family members so the often-complicated issues discussed in seminars can be processed with loved ones. A case study shows the benefits of family involvement and discussion of a retirement-related problem stresses the need to involve one's family in decision-making.

▧ Useful Web Sites

Brandt, Avrene L. 2008. "Transition issues for the elderly and their families." http://www.ec-online.net/knowledge/Articles/brandttransitions.html.

Gilly, Mary, Hope Schau, and Mary Wolfinbarger. 2008. "Seniors and the Internet: Consuming Technology to Enhance Life and Family Involvement." http://www.crito.uci.edu/noah/HOIT/HOIT%20Papers/Seniors%20and%20the%20Internet.pdf.

Marriage and Family Encyclopedia. 2008. Retirement Influences on Marital and Family Relations. http://family.jrank.org/pages/1406/Retirement-Retirement-Influences-on-Marital-Family-Relations.html.

Steiner, Sheyna. 2008. "Is retirement different for women?" http://biz.yahoo.com/brn/080820/26045.html?.v=1.

Walcott, Illene. 2008. "Older worker, families and public policy." *Family Matters,* No.53, Winter 1999: 77–81. http://www.aifs.gov.au/institute/pubs/fm/fm53iw2.pdf.

▧ References

Carpenter, B. D., K. Rickdeschel, K. S. Van Haitsma, and P. H. Feldman. December 2006. "Adult children as informants about parent's psychosocial preferences." *Family Relations* 55:552–63.

Glaser, K., R. Stuchbury, C. Tomasine, and J. Askham, J. 2008. "The long-term consequences of partnership dissolution for support in later life in the United Kingdom." *Aging & Society* 329–351.

Hershey, D. A., J. C. Mowen, and J. M. Jacobs-Lawson. 2003. "An experimental comparison of retirement planning intervention seminars." *Educational Gerontology* 339–359.

Nuttman-Schwartz, O. April/June 2007. *Families in Society* 88(2): 192–202.

Pienta, A. M. 2003. "Partners in marriage: An analysis of husbands' and wives' retirement behavior." *Journal of Applied Gerontology* 22:340.

Shu, Elizabeth. 2005. "Elder or Dependent Adult Abuse." *Psychology Today.* http://psychologytoday.com/conditions/elderabuse.html.

Turner, M. J., W. C. Bailey, and J. P. Scott. 1994. "Factors influencing attitude toward retirement and retirement planning among midlife university employees." *Journal of Applied Gerontology* 13:143–56.

14 ■ ■ ■

Making the Retirement Decision

A number of researchers confirm that making the decision to retire can be very difficult. Although it is often assumed that retirement is a pleasant experience, and for many people it is, the process itself can be daunting and the decision itself so difficult to make that about 30 percent of all retirees perceive it as being very stressful (Atchley, 1975; Bossé, Aldwin, Levenson, and Workman-Daniels, 1991; Braithwaite, Gibson, and Bosly-Craft, 1986).

Reasons for retirement stress include forced retirement, worker burnout and job unhappiness, a belief that a new job will be just as unrewarding and stressful as a current position, early retirement, retirement due to ill health, and financial difficulties. Forced retirement or retirement in which workers are given strong messages that they are unwanted have both been associated with greater difficulties adjusting (Atchley, 1982; Walker, Kimmel, and Price, 1981), lower satisfaction with retirement (Isaksson, 1997), adverse psychological reactions (Sharpley and Layton, 1998), and increased stress (Isaksson, 1997; Sharpley and Layton, 1998).

Individuals who are forced to retire because of ill health predictably report lower levels of morale (Braithwaite et al., 1986), higher stress scores (Bossé et al., 1991), and are at greater risk for emotional difficulties (Sharpley and Layton, 1998). Martin Mathews and Brown (1988) found that the lower the socioeconomic status of men, the more negative the impact of retirement overall, often because of a lack of planning, lower post-retirement income, early health problems, and few alternatives to work. Also, individuals who experience a substantial loss of income during retirement tend to experience poor morale (Richardson and Kilty, 1991) and poor adjustment (Palmore, Fillenbaum, and George (1984). Many people who find their retirement plans changed because companies no longer honor pension plans or have grossly changed pension plans also report lower satisfaction with retirement and greater levels of stress.

Fletcher and Hansson (1991) report that retirees who expected to have very little personal control over their lives during retirement not only had more negative views of retirement, but also feared the event. Glamser (1976) found that those expecting retirement to be a positive experience held a positive attitude about retirement, while those expecting retirement to be a negative adjustment held negative attitudes.

Early retirement is a complex issue for many older adults who may feel diminished and mistreated at work and see retirement as a way of coping with low morale and stress. Often it isn't a solution, since many early retirees have not thought through retirement as a lifestyle change and may still desire to work in new organizations but may believe that their age makes new employment unlikely. Financial incentive plans for early retirement that seem lucrative may in fact offer a person less financial security in the long run and reduced social security and pension benefits. Work is important to most people because it offers status and a daily schedule. When those two factors are taken away, many early retirees feel unimportant and confused about how to spend their day. As a nurse told a colleague when he began chatting about his plan to retire early, "You have 30 good years ahead of you," she said. "What are you going to do with yourself?" She was absolutely right, and our colleague decided to handle his unhappiness with a current job by finding another job elsewhere, and it gave him two more years of work while he began careful planning for retirement and increased his savings.

Mor-Barak and Tynan (1993) suggest that retirement at 65 is an "artifact of the Social Security laws that has acquired certain conveniences, leading to its perception and adoption as 'normative'" (p. 49). They also says that it "enables employers to dispense with the services of older workers gracefully, avoiding the administrative difficulties of selectively firing often 'faithful' workers" (p. 49) while allowing older workers to "salvage" self-respect because retiring at a specific age means you are a member of a class of workers who were let go by mandate from the workforce rather than being individually removed. However, they write:

> [T]hese conveniences do not mean that the current retirement system is beneficial for everyone. Retirement, which was once seen as a great

achievement for the worker, is now viewed as an obstacle by people who feel they can and want to continue participating in the work force. Improved health and longer life expectancy prolong the period in which older adults can be productive in society. In addition, the larger variety of jobs not demanding physical strength enables more older people to continue working. These changes call for policy alterations to provide older adults with options and real choices with respect to work and retirement. (Mor-Barak and Tynan, 1993, p. 49)

Maestas and Li (2007) consider what happens to workers who retire early because of burnout. They write that because burnout rises with continued exposure to stress at work, it should peak just prior to retirement, then decline after the individual leaves the workplace. An individual for whom burnout is high enough to induce retirement may later un-retire if he or she experiences boredom and believes that returning to work will outweigh any negative consequences of working. This notion of un-retiring should help many older workers experiencing burnout to realize that the desire to work often returns in time, and that retirement decisions based entirely on burnout may suggest that leaves of absence, requests for work assignment changes, and cycling over to other types of work may be alternatives to retirement. Keep in mind that it may be more difficult to return to work, at least stimulating work, after you retire because breaks in a work record are often felt by employers to be a bad sign.

An Example

Jason Stewart is a 63-year-old professor of counseling at a lower-level public university in the Midwest. He has been feeling burned out and unhappy about his job, believing that the students he trains are inferior and that most students have lost their idealism and only want to be private practitioners and make a great deal of money. He chose counseling as a career to help others and to make the world a better place—ideas that seem old-fashioned in the current climate of cynicism and narcissism that he finds among the students he teaches. His feelings of burnout and unhappiness have been gaining in strength since Jason was passed over for the chairmanship of his department five years ago. He is now wondering if he should quit work completely or seek another job, and has come for retirement counseling to help him decide on a course of action. Jason has no hobbies other than reading mysteries, watching films, and writing articles and books. He wants the counselor to use a brief problem-solving approach that focuses on the present, doesn't assume that a problem has its origins in the past, and uses logical solutions.

The initial sessions went very well. Jason was highly motivated, did a great deal of reading about early retirement and older adult burnout, and found that it wasn't unusual for people in his field to feel burned out and unhappy with their jobs after many years of tough, loyal, and successful work without very much financial or emotional payoff. As Jason read, talked to the counselor, and made behavioral charts, he began to complain about feeling depressed. "I still don't know what to do," he said, and wondered if the counselor had any suggestions. He did. Why not enter the job market and see if he could find a job where his skills could be put to better use and where the students were stronger?

Jason did just that, and much to his surprise he was a finalist for several very high-level positions at highly ranked universities. He spoke to the counselor about the experience. "I wanted something better, but now I'm scared. I don't think I want to work that hard, and I'm worried that having been in a mediocre university makes me unprepared to deal with high-level faculty and students. The thought of moving makes me feel old and tired."

The counselor listened to Jason for several sessions as he discussed his confusion and concerns about his job possibilities. She told him that it seemed as if the pull to stay was stronger than the pull to leave. Was there a way he could stay at his university and perhaps change what he was doing and begin to work less? Jason explored these options and came back with an idea:

> I found out that we have an early retirement plan where you can get your pension and Social Security and still work for five years up to 50 percent of the time and get paid using your current salary and benefit levels as a base. At the end of the five-year period, you can work part-time but at a lower salary rate. I think I could do that, and maybe it would help me deal with retirement. The problem is that I don't want to keep teaching, so I went to my chair and discussed the plan. He wants me to spend the 50 percent time creating new curricula and trying to deal with the problem of too many poor students in the department. He doesn't think we have enough diversity and he wants to see more idealistic students and faculty. Everyone was feeling the same way I did, he told me, which was a great surprise to me. He said that the reason I was passed over for the chair's position had nothing to do with me or the faculty. The faculty wanted me but the administration wanted someone younger. It pissed me off to find out about ageism, but I had originally thought it was because they didn't like me. Having five years to ease myself into retirement would give me time to write books and to do some traveling. I live alone, and maybe it's time to find someone who can offer companionship and intimacy. I've put off those needs since I divorced 20 years ago, and I feel very lonely at times.

The counselor thought his idea was a good one and wondered how he might find someone to be in his life. "I was reading a mystery novel by the Swedish writer Henning Mankell called *Firewall* (1998)," he said. "His main character, a cop called Kurt Wallander, is like me: lonely and set in his ways but in need of someone in his life. The detective uses a dating service and finds someone. I started thinking about women who have given me some indication that they are interested in me. Maybe I'll just follow up and see if I can find someone that way. I don't think I could ever use a dating service at my age, so we'll see. And I need to start going to our national conferences. I met my wife that way and we did pretty well for almost 20 years; not bad in this day and age."

Our Advice on When to Retire

We think you should keep on working until doing so is no longer an option. It helps if you can phase into retirement gradually. It also helps if you have a good idea that you'll be able to handle spare time and a schedule that doesn't include work to fill up your day. We think extended vacations, leaves of absence, and part-time work before retirement can help you determine this. If you have a date in mind when you are planning to retire, then you should get as much information about your pension plans, Social Security, and investments as you can to anticipate if retirement will be financially feasible. We suggest you start doing this at least two years before you plan to retire. Many people find the initial information about pension plans and social security a little hard to understand. The more time you have to understand your financial future, the better you'll be able to decide if your plan is reasonable or if a little more time might be needed. That means drawing up a realistic budget and factoring in yearly cost-of-living increases. We'll show you how to do that in the next few chapters. We've explained investing and how much you'll need to live a comfortable life. We think that information is accurate. Don't try and lowball that estimate only to find out that you need more income once you've retired. It's easier to keep working than to retire and find a comparable job.

You should attend as many pre-retirement seminars as possible because each time you attend you'll probably learn something new, and you should have serious discussions with your loved ones to make certain they support your decision, particularly your spouse if you're married. Being around someone a lot more than either of you is used to can cause marital conflict. You might also talk to your retired friends and get their read on when to retire, although it's clearly a personal decision and only you can decide when the time is right.

We're going to talk about a lot of other issues in future chapters, such as where to live and how to develop new careers and work projects. You should certainly think seriously about everything related to the decision and then remember that most retired people go through stages and that one of the stages is regret. Many retired people retire and then un-retire.

One of our friends told us that it's absolutely true that you do regret leaving full-time work, but in time, when you get things settled in your life and have enough to keep you fully active, retirement is all about independence. It's a wonderful state to be in because you, not your job, your career, or anyone else, control your own destiny. The mix of leisure time, some work, family activities, volunteerism, travel, further education, and fulfilling your dreams can provide a mix that is just plain intoxicating.

The decision to retire can be hard to make and the timing may not be completely right, but we're only human, and we can't know for sure how any decision works out. That's why you'll need to have a fallback position if you find that retirement is not working for you. Agreements to let you return to your job, new careers, and new work projects—all are fallback positions and you should take some time before you retire to develop them carefully.

Summary

In this chapter we discuss the many conflicting feelings and emotions that contribute to retirement anxiety and suggest ways of coping so you can make the best decision possible. Even when that takes place, many retirees go through a short period of regret, which disappears as they become more comfortable with the many benefits of retired living. Challenging work often provides opportunity for second careers and part-time work and much more leisure time to read, travel, become involved with community, and pursue personal interests and hobbies. The more planning you've done to develop a time to retire that is right for you, the more you will be able to transition to meaningful activities in retirement.

■ Useful Web Sites

About.com. 2008. Do I Really Want to Retire? 2008. http://retireplan.about.com/od/caniretire/a/want_to_retire.htm.

Beesley, Scott. 1997. "Spousal Influence on the Decision to Retire." http://www.economica.ca/ew02_1p3.htm.

Berger, Leslie. "When Do You Retire? Here Are 6 Answers." *New York Times*, March 21, 2001, http://www.geocities.com/TheTropics/Shores/5315/nytimes.html.

McCune, Joseph T., and Neal Schmitt. 1980. "The Relationship between Job Attitudes and the Decision to Retire." Paper presented at the Annual Meeting of the Midwestern Psychological Association, St. Louis, Missouri, May 1–3. http://eric.ed.gov/ERICDocs/data/ericdocs2sql/content_storage_01/0000019b/80/34/3d/2b.pdf.

Seniors Resources Onlines. When do you plan to retire? http://www.community.wa.gov.au/DFC/Communities/Seniors/Retirement+Planning/Planning_an_Active_Retirement.htm.

■ References

Atchley, R. C. 1975. "Adjustment to the loss of job at retirement." *International Journal of Aging and Human Development* 6:17–27.

Atchley, R. C. 1982. "Retirement: Leaving the world of work." *Annals of the American Academy of Political and Social Sciences* 464:120–31.

Bossé, R., C. M. Aldwin, M. R. Levenson, and K. Workman-Daniels. 1991. "How stressful is retirement? Findings from the Normative Aging Study." *Journal of Gerontology* 46:9–14.

Braithwaite, V. A., D. M. Gibson, and R. Bosly-Craft. 1986. "An exploratory study of poor adjustment styles among retirees." *Social Science and Medicine* 23:493–99.

Fletcher, W. L., and R. O. Hansson. 1991. "Assessing the social components of retirement anxiety." *Psychology and Aging* 6:76–85.

Glamser, F. D. 1976. "Determinants of a positive attitude toward retirement." *Journal of Gerontology* 31:104–07.

Isaksson, K. 1997. "Patterns of adjustment to early retirement." *Reports from the Department of Psychology* 828:1–13. Stockholm, Sweden: Stockholm University.

Maestas, N., and X. Li. October 2007. Burnout and retirement decision. Michigan Retirement Research Center, University of Michigan.

Martin Matthews, A., and K. H. Brown. 1988. "Retirement as a critical life event." *Research on Aging* 9:548–71.

Mor-Barak, M. E., and M. Tynan. January 1993. "Older workers and the workplace: A new challenge for occupational social work." *Social Work* 38(1):45–55.

Palmore, E. B., G. G. Fillenbaum, and L. K. George. 1984. "Consequences of retirement." *Journal of Gerontology* 39:109–16.

Richardson, V. E., and K. M. Kilty. 1991. "Adjustment to retirement: Continuity vs. discontinuity." *International Journal of Aging and Human Development* 33:151–69.

Sharpley, C. F., and R. Layton. 1998. "Effects of age of retirement, reason for retirement and pre-retirement training on psychological and physical health during retirement." *Australian Psychologist* 33:119–24.

Walker, J., D. Kimmel, and K. Price. 1981. "Retirement style and retirement satisfaction: Retirees aren't all alike." *International Journal of Clinical Psychology* 41:58–62.

Part IV

NEW COMMUNITIES AND SINGLE LIFE

Chapters 15 and 16 discuss new communities and single life after retirement. Many people look forward to moving to warmer climates after they retire. Retirement communities have flourished as a consequence, but they are not for everyone. Chapter 15 discusses the positives and negatives of retirement communities and gives some suggestions on what to look for in a community before you move. Chapter 16 discusses single retired life. Most people who are single and retire—and there are many more retired singles than we would have guessed—are very satisfied with their lives. Loneliness is a problem for some, and Chapter 16 considers ways of preventing feelings of loneliness and isolation for retired singles.

15 ▪ ▪ ▪

Moving to a New Community

There are a number of wonderful places to live after you retire. If you can afford it, moving to a new community with a milder climate or lower costs of living is always a consideration. So is staying put and spending the part of the year with bad weather somewhere else. In this chapter we will consider the pros and cons of moving, staying where you are, retirement communities, and what the experts say about the best places to retire.

▪ Retirement Communities

There are a number of wonderful retirement communities in the United States. It's not our purpose to tell you which one is best for you (we've included a Web site with the 100 best planned communities at the end of the chapter, but we don't endorse it, and list it only for your convenience), but we *will* discuss issues to consider in selecting a community, and some information about retirement communities from the research literature to help you select the one that's best for you. As Streib (2002) writes, "Retirement communities can be havens for many older people because they offer services, transportation, security, activities, social activities, neighborliness, that many older adults want and need" (p. 4).

A retirement community is often defined as one where you or your spouse must be 55 or over. The reality is that younger families sometimes live in retirement communities with their older parents. Some communities limit the stay to 60 days, but we hear that it's a rule that's not often enforced. You need to check with the community administration if you consider this to be a problem and do some drive-bys to see if there are children out in any numbers in the late afternoon and early evening.

Retirement communities often have an amazing number of activities, including golf, tennis, swimming, gyms, hiking trails, clubs of every type, and social events that help you meet other residents. You will be charged a fee paid to the homeowners association (HOA) for all of these extra facilities. It's usually fairly inexpensive ($100–200 or less), but beware of new communities where the builder supports the HOA to keep fees low. We hear of communities every day that have to substantially raise HOA fees because the builder has only committed to subsidizing the community for a limited period of time or because of bankruptcy. Fees then go up dramatically. Be sure to find out the stability of fees and repair and renovation projects that may increase fees, such as swimming pool or tennis court renovations. In some communities HOA dues cover repairs of the outside of your home or condo. If massive repairs of roofs are needed, this can dramatically raise your HOA fees or result in a large one-time assessment.

Retirement communities sometimes have problems with management companies that do a poor job, so look at the management company record before you select a community. If management companies change often, it could mean an overly demanding or intrusive HOA board of directors or a poorly functioning board that provides little oversight. Both spell trouble.

Lapsley (2001) found that residents of retirement communities with a need to dominate and control others sometimes gravitate to important leadership positions, where they tend to enforce rigid rules that are very annoying to others. He writes, "The primary pattern of over-controlling is seen in the exploitation of leadership positions in community organizations. . . . Some over-controllers in leadership roles are also quite vindictive, seeking retribution or revenge (unlimited 'payback') against those whom they perceive to have slighted them" (p. 446). It's important to determine if this is true of a board of directors of a community you may want to live in, how long people serve on boards, and whether there are ways to oust particularly difficult people. As Streib (2002) points out, "The marketing programs of retirement communities never mention that a variety of disagreements may arise and some of these may take on considerable importance" (p. 6).

One of the ways retirement communities are able to offer fairly low rates for homes is that the basic homes without views are cheap, but premiums are charged for better lots. These premiums may increase the price of a moderately priced home from $5,000 to $100,000 or more. A basic lot may have a lovely view of the side of someone's house and the roofs of others. There is also the issue of upgrades that can be particularly expensive and unnecessary, or that can be done privately for less money. What may begin as an inexpensive house can escalate into something beyond your means, so have a financial plan and stick to it.

Not everyone likes to be around older people all of the time. People in retirement communities tend to talk a lot about their health. If you find health talk boring or depressing, retirement communities may not be for you. Some communities have an average age that is considerably older than you are. You may want to find this out if you prefer to be around people closer to your age. There is talk about people increasingly forming ghettos with others who are like them in political leanings and social beliefs. We think this is true, and speaking personally about the community in which we live, often mentioned as a top-ten place to retire, the deeply conservative and sometimes bigoted beliefs of many retirees can be a major annoyance. You should try to get a sense of the social and political leanings of the people in the community and find out if there are clusters of people with whom you are more likely to interact.

Check out the community when the weather is at its worst. There is nothing like being in Sun City, Arizona, in the summer when it's 115 degrees, the humidity is high from the summer monsoon rains, and the streets are absolutely vacant to give one a sense of the other side of desert living—the side you won't see during the beautiful desert winters. Some people we know have taken extended vacations and stayed in retirement communities to get more of a sense of whether it's for them. We think this is a very good idea. Many retirement communities have furnished rentals for this exact reason.

Don't by fooled by retirement communities that advertise low taxes. Many states with no income tax make up for it with high property and sales taxes. Texas, which has no income tax, has communities like San Antonio that charge a 2.5–3.5 percent property tax on the assessed value of a home. For a home with a moderate assessed value of $250,000, that could mean a property tax as high as $8,750 a year. Communities in some states have added an additional state sales tax to an existing state sales tax, which can bring the tax up to 10 percent or more on nonessential items such as clothing, cars, and any nonfood or medication purchase. Sales taxes are regressive in that people with less income pay a much greater proportion of their income in sales taxes than more affluent people do. This is particularly true of retirees on fixed budgets. It is also true that you get what you pay for. States with low taxes are often service-poor in many areas that are essential to older adults, including public transportation.

Finally, a retirement community should have available medical services nearby. Some new communities don't. This can present a major problem for the retiree who doesn't want to drive long distances, has problems navigating urban freeways, or has health issues that require immediate care. The same is true of other services such as shopping. We especially like communities that have nearby shopping that is easily available by golf cart or shuttle. Given the price of gas, driving a long distance to shop can wreak havoc with your budget.

■ Best Communities for Retirees

Many national magazines have articles each year listing the best places to retire. We are amazed to find on this list places where it is cold and the weather is miserable much of the year. We don't know why a community is listed, but you're welcome to read these lists and even visit them to see for yourself. We find it hard to understand how lists can change each year, and suspect that the articles are written with less than stellar research. Frankly, the only way to find out about a place is to spend time there. Our hometown of Prescott, Arizona, was one of *Money Magazine*'s top five places to retire in 2006. It's a great place, we think, but not without its flaws. You'd have to live here a while to know that we have an extreme doctor shortage and that the average age in the county we live in is 60, which means that a large number of older people with medical problems tax an already weak medical system. Winters are cold—we get snow and sleet, and the summers are hot and wet. During spring and fall, we occasionally have forest fires and back burning by the Forest Service that pollutes the air. Therefore, if you have asthma it's not a good place to live. Retirees in Prescott are very politically conservative, which makes political conversations difficult if you happen to be more liberal. Nobody would call Prescott the cultural hub of the country or, for that matter, Phoenix, a two-hour drive away. It's nice to see so much natural beauty, but sometimes you hunger for a cultural event after tales told by the cowboy storytellers at the Palace Bar begin to grow stale. It's also a complacent place and more than a few people have told us that they've lost the desire to travel and explore because Prescott is just too comfortable.

On the other hand, property taxes are fairly low, the cost of living is moderate, there are 450 miles of hiking trails through some incredibly beautiful country, and housing is still relatively inexpensive if you don't mind living 5–10 miles from downtown. There are numerous free events on the square in downtown Prescott every summer weekend. We have a very nice Costco where there are no lines, and a surprisingly large number of national stores for such a small community. Restaurants are plentiful, people are warm and friendly, and truth be told, we wouldn't trade it for anywhere else—well, maybe a condo on the southern California coast or a chalet in Aspen. Even with the best of information, adjusting to a new community is a personal thing. You find people who complain about our community and everything we think is good about it. We tend to think of them as malcontents, but when you listen to them closely you hear that it's a lonely place for singles, that it's too dominated by politicians looking out for their own self-interest, and that it's not progressive enough in ways that help older adults with their needs. As with much of the Southwest, public transportation is inadequate to nonexistent.

The point is that what's wonderful for you may be awful for someone else. You can read the lists of best retirement communities and look, but don't take anyone's word for it. Be an active and skeptical consumer. As Pullium Weston (2008) writes, "Every location has its drawbacks, a point that's often missed by those dreaming of a brand new life in a new place. Those who move to escape their problems will probably find their issues migrated with them; as the saying goes, 'Wherever you go, there you are.' Anyway, if there were a real Shangri-la, we'd all move there and wreck it with congestion" (p. 1).

■ Staying Put

As we noted in an earlier chapter, people over 65 are much less likely to move than younger people. Home is where one has memories of family, it's comfortable, probably less expensive, and close to friends, your doctor, and your handyman. You have a sense of community that's missing when you move to a new community. Furthermore, your family is probably close by, and staying put is a lot less stressful than moving, which is so stressful that many people avoid the experience altogether. Streib (2002) points out that, on the face of it, retirement communities have a strong attraction for many older adults. He wonders why more people don't move from their homes after retirement and responds by saying, "A major reason is that 'aging in place' has certain psychological benefits. It is easier for the person to remain in a familiar, comfortable place. Moving involves making difficult choices of reducing one's possessions that have been collected over a lifetime" (p. 4).

Many retirees consider living overseas because the cost of living is cheap, but on close examination discover that a low cost of living may be offset by travel costs, lack of good medical care, and security issues. We know Mexico well, and ads saying that you can live on a shoestring in Mexico are highly misleading and often untrue. Mexico in many ways is just as expensive and, in some instances, more expensive than the United States, and laws we take for granted are often not available to protect American homebuyers.

These are all good reasons to consider staying put when you retire, but it doesn't mean you can't or shouldn't explore other areas of the country, or even live elsewhere part of the year. Many people rent during bad weather months and find that living in several places where they can get the best of the weather all year is ideal. We will talk about second homes in another section of the book (we're not very positive about second homes from a financial point of view), but renting opens the door to living in many different places and exploring this beautiful country of ours. And it's also reasonable. There are a number of Web sites where you can find good vacation or monthly rentals, and there are opportunities to house swap. At the end of this chapter, we provide a few Web sites you might want to take a look at.

■ Moving to a New Community: A Personal Story

Patricia and I met when I was about to turn 65 and she was about to turn 60. I'm a retired university professor, and Patricia was a legal secretary working for a large international law firm in Los Angeles. We began dating while I rented a condo in Palm Springs and she lived in West Los Angeles. After a few months of commuting, I was spending more and more time with her. We thought it was silly and expensive to maintain two homes, and seven months after we met I moved into her condo in West Los Angeles.

Both of us are from the Midwest and neither of us liked Los Angeles, but we love the West and wanted to retire here. We spent the next year and a half using every opportunity to check out potential places to retire. When my daughter graduated from the University of Arizona, we checked out Tucson and Las Cruces, New Mexico, two places experts suggest are good places to retire. We found Tucson much too hot and spread out, and Las Cruces a bit too small and isolated. We also spent three days in Boise, Idaho, a place I'd lived in for a year, but couldn't find affordable housing near the center of the city. We also found it much more congested than it had been three years earlier. We spent a weekend visiting friends of Pat's in Portland, Oregon, and found it a great place to live, but also dreary and wet. We looked at communities in California such as San Luis Obispo, a wonderful place, but it was expensive beyond comprehension. We were pretty sure we wanted to live in a smaller community, but one with amenities, which was also safe, had good weather, and a local college. We also wanted to live close enough to a big city so we could have good medical care if we needed something beyond the expertise of the local community, travel on less expensive flights, and enjoy the benefits of urban life without having to endure the liabilities.

I knew about Prescott from my days of teaching at Arizona State University (ASU) in Tempe. When we finally went to Prescott on what I called one of our "scouting trips," we spent three days with an excellent real estate agent we'd found online, couldn't find a house we liked, but found the community very appealing. We originally went in August when Prescott can be very warm and wet, but found that it didn't bother us. We returned in February of the next year, feeling some pressure to find something and sell Patricia's condo before the real estate bubble burst in Los Angeles. Our real estate agent sent us a number of homes to look at on the Internet before we came. Fortunately, we found an exceptional house at a fair price, which is very comfortable and appealing at a fraction of the cost in Los Angeles. Patricia was able to sell her condo before the bubble burst completely and made a nice profit. We moved to Prescott in May 2007 and like it in ways that only people who have lived in congested and impersonal places can understand.

Do we miss the big city? Not a bit. Phoenix is plenty big enough, and I drive there once a week to teach at ASU. Although I enjoy the day, that's enough big city life for me. Is Prescott too small? No. We joined the local tennis club, play often and have made some great friends, some of them a lot younger than we are. We stay very busy. Are there other places we might have found that we might like better? Perhaps, but that's for another day. Right now we're content, busy, happy, and healthy. What more could we ask for? -MDG

▨ Summary

This chapter discusses the issues of where to live after you retire. Most people stay in their homes or move nearby to be close to extended family and their physicians and other professionals with whom they've worked for long periods of time. For those who want the many benefits of retirement community living, we suggest spending time at the community of choice during bad parts of the season, that you speak to as many members of the community as possible, and that you understand the pricing system retirement communities use where homes are priced reasonably but you pay a significant premium for lots with views. Other considerations include closeness to doctors and shopping; since retirement communities may be a distance from either, this is an issue that shouldn't be ignored.

▨ Useful Web Sites

Ahern, Bill. Low Tax States? Think Again. http://www.heartland.org/Article.cfm?
    artId=166
America's Top 100 Best Master-Planned Retirement Communities. http://www.
    retirenet.com/top100
Home Swapping. http://www.homeexchange.com
Vacation Rentals by Owners. http://www.vrbo.com
Vacation Rentals. http://www.vacationrentals.com

CNN.Money.com: Best Places to Retire by Level of Education, Health Care, Cost of Living, and many other indicators. http://money.cnn.com/magazines/moneymag/bpretire/2006/top25s/educated.html

▓ References

Lapsley, J. N. 2001. "Overcontrol in retirement communities." *Pastoral Psychology* 49(6).

Pulliam Weston, L. 2008. "Home sweet home: The hottest place to retire." http://articles.moneycentral.msn.com/RetirementandWills/RetireInStyle/HomeSweetHomeTheHottestPlaceToRetire.aspx.

Streib, G. F. 2002. "An introduction to retirement communities." *Research on Aging* 24:3.

16 ■ ■ ■

Single and Retired

It's not unusual to worry about being single and retired. There are a number of commonly held beliefs that single people are lonelier than married people, have more illnesses at an earlier point in their retirement, are more unhappy than their married counterparts, and enjoy life less. A brief look at some of the literature on retired singles confirms these popular beliefs. For example, Gamm (2008) writes about the fear of emotional loneliness and "the lack of someone to share dinner with in the evenings, someone to share time with on the weekend, and someone to look after you when you are not well" (p. 1). Gamm writes:

> Becoming single can simplify and complicate the issues of retirement. First, you now only have yourself to think about—no in-laws to worry about, no worrying about your partner's health. You basically can do what you want to do! Conversely, you now don't have a partner to share things with or for emotional support. It means being deprived of the comfort of a partner and possibly may mean isolation and loneliness.

While these concerns may be true for some retired singles, and loneliness is certainly everything it's cracked up to be, there are a number of single retired men and women who live well, are happy and healthy, and are anything but lonely. This chapter is about ways to enjoy retirement and to be socially involved with and without a partner. Many of us do it and thrive.

▦ Loneliness and Older Adults

Hawkley and Cacioppo (2007) note the relationship between loneliness and more rapid declines in health than in older adults who are not lonely, supporting a popular belief that loneliness is a destructive force in our lives and older adults who are lonely (and without a partner) are particularly likely to suffer health problems because of the association between loneliness and depression. However, they also report that there are few actual well-done pieces of research to support this contention and very few studies showing higher rates of loneliness for single older adults. Married couples can experience loneliness as a result of shifts in the relationship and empty nest syndrome. Interestingly, Hawkley and Cacioppo (2007) write that in their research, having friends and other social contacts can reduce and even eliminate loneliness in the absence of a partner. The authors also note that loneliness is a progressive condition. If you are lonely before you retire, it's possible that loneliness will carry over into retirement unless you do something about it before and after you retire.

There are a number of reasons we feel lonely. For some of us, loneliness is a life-long condition having a great deal to do with our early life experiences. Children who fail to bond with troubled parents often experience lifelong loneliness. This type of loneliness needs the assistance of a very good mental health professional, since people with lifelong feelings of loneliness often do not report lessened feelings of loneliness even when they are in relationships, with friends, or in social situations. Others feel lonely in later life as a result of a divorce or the end of a long-term relationship. And yet others begin to experience loneliness as the result of the death of parents or declining health. All of these situations should be thought of as serious indicators of the need for professional help. Merely increasing your social contacts works for a number of people, but when it doesn't work, you need to put your pride aside and seek good professional help.

There are other reasons for feeling lonely, many of which have to do with being discounted as we age. Our society is a youth-oriented society that assumes older adults have less to contribute as they age. This form of ageism often drives perfectly capable older adults from jobs they do well and makes them believe that their productive lives are over once they reach retirement age. Rokach and Neto (2005) found a significant difference in a Canadian population in which culture was factored into the measure of loneliness. Older adults from traditional cultures in which age is considered a sign of wisdom are far less likely to feel lonely than those from the normative culture in North America. Many social scientists believe that an important reason older adults may experience more loneliness is that they've been marginalized by a culture that defines them as nonproductive and noncontributing. Older single adults who have been downsized or forced from jobs because of age are more likely to experience loneliness in retirement because a prime place to form friendships is in the workplace.

One of the mistakes that older single men and women make is to load up their lives with activities and people with whom they have superficial relationships. Granted, it's better to be socially active than not, but when people are really in need because of a crisis, superficial friendships are almost always disappointing. One older single woman told us that when she injured her leg in a car accident and was homebound for many months, she had almost no visitors or phone calls from the many people she thought were good friends—obviously, they weren't. A retired single man told us that in the midst of a severe episode of rapid heartbeat he could not stop, he called a lady with whom he thought he had a strong relationship who told him to call an ambulance because she didn't want to spend time at the hospital waiting for him. There is a quantum difference between a friend you can count on and an acquaintance you can't.

When the elements of good friendships were evaluated by age, Schnittker (2007) found that older adults expect agreeableness in their friends, or the ability to get along. Not surprisingly, the researchers also found that a person's concept of what constitutes a good friendship is highly related to one's view of the quality of the relationship he or she had with parents. The researchers also found that we base our concept of friendships on the early messages given to us by parents about our friends. Favorable feedback about friends at an early age can have a lasting impact on whom we consider to be friendship material.

Parents discuss issues of friendship with children and help us define the attributes of friendships. One single older adult we know said that his mother's favorite expression was "better a good friend nearby than a family member far away." What she meant was that we often rely on friends more than family. For our friend's mother, friendship was a serious commitment to others. In some ways it was like being committed to a spouse because it implied high expectations of a friend. Needless to say, these high standards for friendship brought a good deal of grief to our friend who told us that he'd been disappointed in people he thought were friends for as long as he could remember. It seems evident that one's definition of friendship has a good deal to do with whether or not we are able to find and retain friends.

While it's easy to say that retired singles should develop a social network of friends and acquaintances, most of us understand that, much as we need intimacy in our lives, we also need friends who allow for emotional openness. When approaching the issue of moving to a new community after retirement, it's important to remember that although friendships transcend distance, it's also vital that we have good friends nearby. To that end, we suggest that you consider the social opportunities available to meet new people in a new community, and the potential to make new friends. We think conversations with other singles can help you determine the opportunities to meet and make friends. And remember that the process takes time. Even with the best information, you still need to attend social functions, interact with others, reach out to people who are likely to be friendship material, and follow through with the social interactions that solidify friendships. False starts are always possible, so don't be discouraged, and remember that just as you are looking for friends, so are others in the community.

A retired single woman we know said that it took her a year after moving to a new community to establish good friendships and to find the places where she could meet other men and women who might also be interested in establishing friendships. She joined a tennis club even though she wasn't a tennis player, learned the game, and has made some very good female friends that way. She often goes to new social events with a new friend because she finds it easier to attend a social event with someone else than face new people alone. At the end of this chapter, we have a list of social, religious, and leisure Web sites that might help you meet other people and begin to form friendships.

▨ Love and Intimacy in a Time of Retirement

Many older adults experience a remarkable renewal of intimacy and come to value a mature notion of love that is more accepting and emotionally healthy than when they were younger. Older love is often more patient. Older adults recognize that the bad times pass and the good times pass. "As you experience the good and bad times, they're more precious, they're richer" (Zernike, 2007, p. 1). It's also true that older people may simply be better able to deal with the emotional aspects of love. As it ages, the brain becomes more programmed to be happy in relationships, according to brain researchers. Zernike adds, "As people get older, they seem to naturally look at the world through positivity and be willing to accept things that when we're young we would find disturbing and vexing" (p. 1).

Regarding older adult intimacy, Stein (2007) reports the results of a study of 3,000 U.S. adults ages 57–85. The study found that half to three-quarters of the respondents remained sexually active, with a "significant population engaging in frequent and varied sex" (p. A1). The study found that physically healthier people reported the highest rates of sexual activity and that a healthy sex life may itself help keep people vibrant. According to Stein, the study noted that 28 percent of the men and 14 percent of the women said sex was very important and those with partners reported being sexually active as often as people in their forties and fifties. "But even among the oldest age group (80–85), 54% of those who were sexually active reported having sex at least two to three times per month and 23% reported having sex once a week or more" (p. A1).

▓ Older Singles and Meeting Intimacy Needs

Almost half of the people 65 and older in the United States are single. According to Perman (2006), many older adults simply date without necessarily wanting to remarry. Living Apart Together (LAT) is a type of relationship in which partners define themselves as a couple, see each other often, but maintain separate residences. Creating this form of relationship may stem from job demands, responsibilities to family members, and so forth, but for others it provides sufficient intimacy but also provides time to see friends, have secure finances, and be involved in activities they enjoy, but which their partners may not. For women, maintaining their own homes constitutes a resource base that provides financial security and avoids comingling finances and the problems that may arise from misunderstandings about money, unequal responsibilities, or broken relationships.

Some states have wisely given older adults the opportunity to have domestic partnerships in which one of the partners might receive the medical benefits of the other. Many people who enter into domestic partnerships have a form of a prenuptial agreement that serves to protect them financially should the relationship end. Entering into a domestic partnership has many of the legal constraints of marriage but fewer of the benefits. Income tax, for example, must be paid as a single taxpayer, and joint returns are disallowed under federal and state guidelines.

Should you use an Internet dating service to meet eligible men and women? There are certainly advantages in that you can control who you meet. However, people often lie about their age or show pictures of themselves that are 10 or even 20 years younger (you shouldn't do this because it offends people when they meet), and some smart but somewhat wacky people can seem healthy online but really aren't in person. One hears that there is a shortage of eligible older men, so for a woman that may make meeting a man more difficult. It's best to have some phone conversations before meeting and then meet somewhere public where the issue of who pays the bill isn't a problem (coffee house, for example). The process can be challenging because not everyone you meet is as nice as they appear online. Just remember that it takes kissing a lot of frogs before you kiss the czar or czarina of the heart. It takes time and patience, but many people find that Internet dating often works amazingly well.

Dating services that have you videotape an interview and then have pictures and bios of men and women you might be interested in often charge $1,500–$3,000 a year. Perhaps there are good ones, but we have heard numerous complaints. Check them out carefully. It might be better just to use Internet dating services that are much cheaper and include members who live in areas you might initially find undesirable because of distance, but who are worth getting to know. Retired people often have a great deal of flexibility in where they can live, and it's a shame to pass up a good person because of distance.

The following personal story may help you understand the challenges and benefits of older love and to realize that older love can provide the same joy you might experience at a younger age but with more lasting results.

■ A Personal Story: Single to Married

We were in our middle fifties when we met by Internet dating. Of course, neither of us knew it then because we were both lying about our ages and had subtracted a neat ten years for purposes of the introductory bio. Each of us thought that the qualities of vitality, sensuality, and sexuality might only be found in someone who was younger.

Casualties of earlier failures, we had both been married and divorced twice. I had been single for five years after concluding a ten-year second marriage that I cheerfully described as "lousy," and David had been out of a marriage for about three years, but was still jointly raising two preteen children. He had a less-than-cordial relationship with his children's mother.

Looking back, I think we had both made similar earlier mistakes in choosing a mate. Certainly, I had opted for physical attraction and sexual activity—not grasping that a lack of complementary intellectual and emotional styles would give rise to the later ever-widening abyss of noncommunication in almost every aspect of daily life. My ex and I really didn't have that much in common, and while we still thought of each other as pretty nice people, we had no real interest or reason to be together. Tired of the emptiness of daily individual pursuits, we parted.

In David's case, he had married a woman almost 19 years his junior. Over time, they were yoked together in a dry, frustrating monotony of daily nonconnection. Ultimately, they parted with pain and rancor and two children to raise in a newly nonconventional family situation.

Each in our own way still yearned for a "final partner." In that person we hoped for compassion, intellect, friendship, mutual values, similar goals, and especially the capacity for a deep, trusting bonding on which to rely. That list was really headed by the unspoken, "I really want to feel excited and sexy (but I don't want to pay the price again for a poor choice)."

For my own part, I'd taken a year off to be with my mother during her waning days and was feeling sad and hurt at her loss. I'd parted ways with a boyfriend who just wasn't available to make the leap to committed loving.

So, for a year, after a friend told me about Internet dating, I dated. I met a lot of very nice men, but not anyone who "turned me on." I realized then that in addition to the more abstract qualities for which I was searching, there was that very essential component called "chemistry." Additionally, I reviewed my past relationships and concluded that they had all begun only on the basis of my definition of "chemistry," and look where they were now!

Later, when David and I had already met and began exchanging thoughts, he too recognized that something in his selection process had also failed.

By the time our paths crossed, David had been dating for over a year and was really jaded. He's a jock kind of guy who doesn't cook for himself and mopes when he's not in a relationship that allows him to be a caretaker. He had seen my bio on the dating site, but had written me off as GU (geographically undesirable). He told me later that he'd found me attractive, but was just too tired and was going to let the ad lapse and spend the rest of his life in a monastic mode. But I contacted him! I'd decided that not only did this man's bio indicate some of the right things, I liked his looks!

David and I exchanged e-mails, then phone calls. But both of us wanted to have an in-person meeting as soon as possible. He did the gentlemanly thing and drove the 40 minutes to my neighborhood. Yes, I know, GU is something that is generally measured in state lines and international boundaries, but this was one fatigued man, and the distance between our little communities looked more like the stretch across the Great Plains than a pleasant tootle along the Southern California coast.

He made it, parking in front of my little house on a Sunday afternoon while I was watering the roses awaiting his arrival. We rushed into one another's arms, pledged our undying troth and have lived happily ever after. Well, not exactly.

David parked in front of my little house, strolled laconically up the driveway, and commenced an hour of being aloof and standoffish. First, he was unfriendly at my pleasant welcome, simply shrugging and maintaining a distance. Then, after entering my house, he looked around and offered, "So? You rent here?"

Sure, I was surprised and somewhat baffled by this diffidence. But patience is a virtue that I'd grown into, and I immediately decided to wait a bit and depend on the earlier long-distance conversations we had shared to show their true colors. I've lived all my life with animals, large and small, and I know that once injured, any animal with any sense is cautious and tentative in returning to try again.

Since that original meeting, we've been together almost 24/7. We did spend the requisite time with beach walks and talks, candlelit dinners, and hand-holding at the movies, but we also almost immediately started meeting real-life issues head-on. These issues had previously triggered old, established patterns in each other, which had led to less-than-happy results in the past.

David had children marching quickly into teen angst. His parenting skills were limited, and mine were nonexistent, as I had never raised children of my own. We clashed on beliefs about conflict resolution and emotional style. We both fell back into patterns—on his part consisting of angry outbursts, and on my part consisting of flight. After a while, I just kept a bag packed. This hurt us both and threatened to break a bond we both wanted to keep. We had periods of comfort and pleasure in each other's company, finding ever more areas in which we shared similar or complementary interests and enjoyments, and devastating eruptions of emotional lava in areas of disagreement. Finally, we got the message. We're too old for this!

By this time we were no longer in our middle fifties—we were both approaching 60. We had to admit to ourselves, and to each other, that time was running out. So we sat down and decided to combine our styles in an effort to attain our mutual goal—happiness together.

We looked at the "big picture," that we continued to be attracted to each other intellectually, emotionally, and sexually. We affirmed that it is the big picture—the company of each other—that is most important, and that continuing the devastating conflict we were experiencing would so damage our little ship of state that it might sink.

So then, what and how to fix the situation? We looked at what we were doing. David was doing anger and I was doing flight. Both activities drove the other person crazy. We looked at where these practices had originated and realized that they were not new to our relationship! David was repeating a pattern learned in early childhood in which his mother had modeled nastiness and vituperation whenever she felt frustration or disappointment. I was still trying to run away from an angry and violent father as I had done when I was a toddler. So we made a conscious decision to declare them "old baggage." It didn't matter exactly where it came from, it just didn't work here. In fact, it hurt more than it helped.

David agreed to modify his pattern of anger by not lashing out at me, and I agreed to put away my suitcases, and to call for a sit-down discussion if a problem came up.

Now, when either of us flips back into some old emotional pattern of disgruntlement, we are committed to recognizing it immediately, acknowledging that it is a pattern, and breaking away from it so as not to damage the other person or the relationship. We simply promised ourselves, and each other, that we would not allow the old misunderstandings of how to treat a significant other to kill our love.

In this way we are affirming, as constantly as possible, our belief in and commitment to the other person and to the relationship that we enjoy. And we do enjoy: In every way, we are kinder to, more entertained by, and accepting of our partner. We are so enriched and comforted by the friendship that continues to grow. Unexpected fallout from our venture is that sensuality and sexuality has been enhanced.

By knowing David better every day, by letting down my own barriers and defenses, I feel safer and less "different" from him. And consequently, I spend more time feeling that we are interacting facets of a "whole," so that touching, sex, listening to each other, and sharing space all become moments of fulfillment and contentment. —CJR

Summary

This chapter discusses single retired life. For many retired singles, life is good and intimacy needs are often met. For some singles, however, life can be lonely, particularly for those who have moved to new communities assuming that they will easily meet other singles. The process of making good friends and the special people who will meet our personal needs as friends or lovers can take time, and the chapter cautions that before you move from a community where you have friends and family, take time to get to know a new community by talking to as many people as possible to decide if that place is for you. The chapter ends with a description of an initially troubled relationship between an older, single couple that moved to something very special.

Great Places to Meet People

1. Osher Lifelong Learning Programs for older adults found at almost all universities, and junior and community colleges. Go to your local university and/or community college to check out programs.
2. Tennis clubs in the United States: http://www.tennismates.com/clubs.asp
3. American Association of University Women: http://www.aauw.org
4. Chamber of Commerce: For listing of local programs go to http://www.chamberofcommerce.com/public/index.cfm?
5. League of Women Voters: http://www.lwv.org/AM/Template.cfm?Section=Home

6. Readers Circle: A listing of local book clubs: http://www.reader-scircle.org
7. Peak to Peak: A comprehensive list of American hiking clubs: http://www.peaktopeak.net/clubs.html
8. Singles organizations for single people. A state-by-state list of singles organizations: http://www.singlesorganizations.com
9. A great Web site for those interested in higher education: Association of Retired Organizations in Higher Education (AROHE): http://www.arohe.org
10. Investopedia: An excellent Web site about investment clubs sponsored by *Forbes* magazine that includes local investment clubs around the country: http://www.investopedia.com/articles/01/062001.asp

▪ References

Gamm, J. 2008. "The social stigma of the retired single female." http://Ezine Articles.com/?expert=Jan_Gamm.

Hawkley, L. C., and J. T. Cacioppo. 2007. "Aging and loneliness: Downhill quickly: Current directions in the psychological sciences." *Association for Psychological Sciences* 16(4): 187.

Perman, D. February 2, 2006. "The changing face of romance in 2006: Are valentines just for the young?" *Intimacy and Aging: Tips for Sexual Health and Happiness. UBC Reports* 52(2).

Rokach, A., and R. Neto. 2005. "Age, culture and the antecedents of loneliness." *Social Behavior and Personality* 33(5): 477–94.

Schnittker, J. 2007. Look (closely) at all the lonely people: Age and the social psychology." *Journal of Aging Health* 19: 659–82.

Stein, R. "Elderly staying sexually active." *The Washington Post*, August 23, 2007, http://www.washingtonpost.com/wp-dyn/content/article/2007/08/22/AR2007 0822 02000_pf.html.

Zernike, K. "Still many-splendored: Love in the time of dementia." *The New York Times*, November 18, 2007, http://www.nytimes.com/2007/11/18/weekinreview/18.

Part V

HEALTH ISSUES

Chapters 17–19 discuss the important issue of health care. Chapter 17 focuses on maintaining good physical and emotional health as we age, while Chapter 18 discusses the complex issue of choosing doctors and knowing which procedures your doctor orders are done for good medical reasons as opposed to protecting the doctor from liability issues. As you will discover, many of the diagnostic procedures and some lab work ordered by doctors in America have little value, are expensive, and may cause unwanted health problems. Insurance and Medicare are discussed in detail so that you understand what Medicare does and does not cover and about the supplementary plans that pay for medical services not covered by basic Medicare. Those plans can be very expensive and add to an already taxed budget. The same plan can cost much more depending on the insurance company, and the wise consumer will shop for the best price and coverage.

Chapter 19 discusses the difficult but prevalent problem of older adult substance abuse, a problem many doctors fail to diagnose, but one that has negative health and mental health consequences. Heavy drinking often begins well before retirement, but for many lonely people it increases during retirement when health problems, loss of a spouse, and loneliness combine to make people very unhappy. This chapter is a must read for those of you who use more than an average and medically wise amount of alcohol on a daily basis.

Chapter 20 is our suggestion for the more spiritual and creative aspects of retirement that really affect retirement satisfaction. We call it "The Road Less Traveled" to suggest that the wonderful aspect of retirement most of us get joy from is the ability to be a free spirit and to go your own way once the constraints of work have been lifted.

17 ▪ ▪ ▪

Staying Healthy

Many of us worry about becoming ill as we age. This chapter discusses preventing or at least significantly delaying some common health problems often associated with aging.

▪ Taking Care of Yourself: Some General Advice

In their research on successful aging, Vaillant and Mukamal (2001) believe that we can identify the predictors of longer and healthier lives before the age of 50 by using the following indicators: (a) parental social class, (b) family cohesion, (c) lack of major depression, (d) ancestral longevity, (e) childhood temperament, and (f) physical health at age 50. Six variables indicating personal control over physical and emotional health that are also related to longer and healthier lives include: (a) absence of alcohol abuse and smoking, (b) the presence of marital/relationship stability, (c) exercise, (d) normal body mass index, (e) positive coping mechanisms, and (f) involvement in continuing education. The authors conclude that we have much greater control over our post-retirement health than had been previously recognized in the literature.

A number of researchers writing about older adults discuss the concept of successful aging. To give you an example of what is meant by successful aging, Vaillant and Mukamal (2001) identify the following indicators: (a) Although elderly people taking three to eight medications a day were seen as chronically ill by their physicians, the cohort deemed to be aging successfully saw themselves as healthier than their peers; (b) elderly adults who age successfully have the ability to plan ahead, and are still intellectually curious and in touch with their creative abilities; (c) successfully aging adults, even those over 95, see life as being meaningful and are able to use humor in their daily lives; (d) aging successfully includes remaining physically active and continuing activities (walking, for example) that were engaged in at an earlier age to remain healthy; (e) older adults who age successfully are more serene and spiritual in their outlook on life than those who age less well; and (f) successful aging includes concern for continued friendships; positive interpersonal relationships; satisfaction with spouses, children, and family life; and social responsibility in the form of volunteer work and civic involvement.

In their research on aging, Vaillant and Mukamal (2001) found that the following contributed to successful aging: (a) Seeking and maintaining quality relationships; (b) having interest and concern for others and being able to give of oneself; (c) having a sense of humor and the ability to laugh and play well into later life; (d) making new friends as we lose older ones— Valiant found that quality friendships have a more positive impact on aging well than retirement income; (e) maintaining desire to learn and to be open to new ideas and new points of view; (f) understanding and accepting our limitations and, when necessary, accepting the help of others; (g) understanding the past and its effect on our lives while living in the present; and (h) focusing on the positives and the good people in our lives rather than on the negative things that may happen to us.

Robert and Li (2001) argue that despite a usual belief in the relationship between higher income in retirement and health, research actually suggests a limited relationship between these two variables. Rather, there seems to be a relationship between living in a healthy community where levels of health are high and one's own health. Lawton (1977) suggests that older adults may experience communities as their primary source of support, recreation, and stimulation, unlike younger adults who find it easier to move about in search of support and recreation. The researchers believe that positive community environments are particularly important to older adults who have health problems that limit their mobility.

Robert and Li (2001) suggest three indicators of healthy communities that directly affect individual health: (a) A physical environment with an absence of noise and traffic, with adequate lighting; (b) an absence of crime, the ability to find safe environments to walk in, and easy access to shopping; and (c) a rich service environment that includes simple and safe access to rapid and inexpensive transportation, the availability of senior centers, and easy access to meal sites. We will keep these indicators of healthy communities in mind when we discuss places to live after retirement.

▓ Preventing Alzheimer's Disease

One of the most disturbing illnesses associated with aging is Alzheimer's disease (AD). Although the risk factors for developing this disease increase as we age, there are promising new data suggesting that it may be possible to limit that risk.

The National Institute for Aging (2006) estimates that as many as 4.5 million Americans suffer from AD. The disease usually begins after age 60, and risk goes up with age. While younger people may also get AD, it is much less common. About 5 percent of men and women ages 65 to 74 have AD, and nearly half of those over the age of 85 may have the disease, with the number of people with the disease doubling every five years beyond age 65. Of the more than 4 million Americans estimated to have an intellectual decline because of AD, one-third have severe dementia and are so impaired that they can no longer manage without assistance in the simplest daily activities, including eating, dressing, grooming, and toileting.

The symptoms of dementia include loss of memory, extreme mood changes, and communication problems, which include a decline in the ability to talk, write, and read. While AD is the most common disease in which dementia is a symptom, people with dementia may suffer from the effects of strokes and heart problems that cause brain damage due to oxygen deprivation. Dementia can also result, to a lesser extent, from the conditions of multiple sclerosis, motor neuron disease, Parkinson's disease, and Huntington's disease.

Brain fitness activities, especially physical activity and aerobic exercise, are believed to protect cognition and benefit memory in midlife (Colcombe et al., 2006). Other studies have found that a revolutionary computer-based program can potentially "revitalize the brain" (George, 2007), and improvements were found in areas of short-term memory and attention among the participants. Carle (2007) discusses several brain-training games such as "Nana" Technology, Posit Science, Mindfit, and MyBrainTrainer.com, in which he describes programs that are "more than just a game" to maintain cognitive strength among older adults. George (2007) states that there is a "life-long ability to adapt, called brain plasticity and the ability to generate new brain cells."

A study published in the *Annals of Neurology* (Scarmeas et al., 2006) suggests that people who eat a "Mediterranean" diet—rich in fruits, vegetables, olive oil, legumes, cereals and fish—have a lower risk of developing AD.

Researchers examined the health and diet of more than 2,000 people over a four-year period. The average age of study participants was 76. None of the participants had AD at the start of the study. By the end of the study, only 260 participants had been diagnosed with AD. Over the course of the study, researchers evaluated how closely participants followed a published definition of the Mediterranean diet. Participants who stuck most closely to the diet were less likely to develop AD than were participants who didn't follow the diet.

Lunde (2008) notes that growing evidence suggests that physical activity may have benefits beyond a healthy heart and body weight. Through the past several years, population studies have suggested that exercise that raises your heart rate for at least 30 minutes several times a week can lower your risk of AD. Physical activity appears to inhibit AD-like brain changes in mice, slowing the development of a key feature of the disease.

In one study, investigators looked at the relationship of physical activity and mental function in about 6,000 women aged 65 and older over an eight-year period. They found that the women who were more physically active were less likely to experience a decline in their mental function than inactive women.

Lunde (2008) reports that Dr. Ronald Petersen, director of the Alzheimer's Research Center at the Mayo Clinic, said on ABC, "Regular physical exercise is probably the best means we have of preventing Alzheimer's disease today, better than medications, better than intellectual activity, better than supplements and diet."

A promising but preliminary study suggests that elderly people who view themselves as self-disciplined, organized achievers may have a lower risk for developing AD than people who are less conscientious (Wilson et al., 2007). According to the researchers, a strong self-directed personality may somehow protect the brain, perhaps by increasing neural connections that can act as a reserve against mental decline. Surprisingly, when the brains of some of the strongly self-directed people in the study were autopsied after their deaths, they were found to have lesions that would meet accepted criteria for AD— even though these people had shown no signs of dementia. The authors point out that prior studies have linked social connections and stimulating activities like working puzzles with a lower risk of AD, while people who experience more distress and worry about their lives are at a higher risk.

At the start of the study, none of the participants (997 older Catholic priests, nuns, and brothers who participated in the Religious Orders Study) showed signs of dementia. The average age was 75. The subjects were given IQ tests and tests to measure self-direction (conscientiousness) and then were tracked for 12 years. Everyone took tests, including a standard personality test, with testing done yearly to determine if there were signs of cognitive decline and dementia. Brain autopsies were performed on most of those who died.

Over the 12 years, 176 people developed AD, but those with the highest scores for "conscientiousness" at the start of the study had an 89 percent lower risk of developing AD, compared to people with the lowest scores for that personality trait. The conscientiousness scores were based on how people rated themselves, on a scale of 0–4, on how much they agreed with statements such as: "I work hard to accomplish my goals," "I strive for excellence in everything I do," "I keep my belongings clean and neat," and "I'm pretty good about pacing myself so as to get things done on time."

When the researchers took into account a combination of risk factors, including smoking, inactivity, and limited social connections, they still found that the conscientious people had a 54 percent lower risk of AD compared to people with the lowest scores for conscientiousness. While these results are very promising because they seem to indicate that people with high expectations of themselves suffer a far less chance of developing AD, it should be noted that the social and physical environments of the subjects (all members of religious communities) contain protective factors that may inhibit or delay the development of AD. Still, this is an exciting study because it suggests that strong personality traits related to conscientiousness should be encouraged and supported in children at early stages of development.

Researchers at the University of North Dakota have been studying the link between diets that are high in fat and the onset of AD. They found that one cup of coffee a day can neutralize the impact of fat on brain functioning, and while the relationship between coffee and AD isn't conclusive, the researchers are optimistic that coffee reduces high levels of iron and cholesterol in the brain that have been associated with AD.

■ Preventing Heart Problems

The following data on heart attacks comes from the American Heart Association (2008):

1. There were 650,000 heart-related deaths in the United States in 2005 (one of every four deaths).
2. There were 1,200,000 new and recurrent coronary attacks per year.
3. About 38 percent of people who experience a coronary attack in a given year die from it.
4. There are 16,000,000 victims of angina (chest pain due to coronary heart disease), heart attack, and other forms of coronary heart disease who are still living (8,700,000 males and 7,300,000 females).
5. From 1994 to 2004, the death rate from coronary heart disease declined 33 percent.

The following information comes from the Mayo Clinic Web site (2008):

1. Don't smoke or use tobacco products

When it comes to heart disease prevention, no amount of smoking is safe. Tobacco smoke contains more than 4,800 chemicals. Many of these can damage your heart and blood vessels, making them more vulnerable to narrowing of the arteries (atherosclerosis). Atherosclerosis can ultimately lead to a heart attack.

In addition, the nicotine in cigarette smoke makes your heart work harder by constricting blood vessels and increasing your heart rate and blood pressure. Carbon monoxide in cigarette smoke replaces some of the oxygen in your blood. This increases your blood pressure by forcing your heart to work harder to supply enough oxygen. Even so-called "social smoking"—only smoking while at a bar or restaurant with friends—is dangerous and increases the risk of heart disease.

The good news, though, is that when you quit smoking, your risk of heart disease drops dramatically within just one year. And no matter how long or how much you smoked, you'll start reaping rewards as soon as you quit.

2. Get active

Regularly participating in moderately vigorous physical activity can reduce your risk of fatal heart disease by nearly 25 percent. And when you combine physical activity with other lifestyle measures, such as maintaining a healthy weight, the payoff is even greater.

Regular physical activity helps prevent heart disease by increasing blood flow to your heart and strengthening your heart's contractions so your heart pumps more blood with less effort. Physical activity also helps you control your weight and can reduce your chances of developing other conditions that may put a strain on your heart, such as high blood pressure, high cholesterol, and diabetes. It also reduces stress, which may also be a factor in heart disease.

Federal guidelines recommend that you get at least 30 to 60 minutes of moderately intense physical activity most days of the week. However, even shorter amounts of activity offer heart benefits, so if you can't meet those guidelines, don't give up. And remember that things like gardening, housekeeping, taking the stairs, and walking the dog all count toward your total. You don't have to exercise strenuously to achieve benefits, but you can see bigger benefits by increasing the intensity, duration, and frequency of your workouts.

3. Eat a heart-healthy diet

Consistently eating a diet rich in fruits, vegetables, whole grains, and low-fat dairy products can help protect your heart. Legumes, low-fat sources of protein, and certain types of fish also can reduce your risk of heart disease. Saturated, polyunsaturated, monounsaturated, and trans fats increase the risk of coronary artery disease by raising blood cholesterol levels. Major sources of saturated fat include beef, butter, cheese, milk, and coconut and palm oils. There's growing evidence that trans fats may be worse than saturated fats because, unlike saturated fats, they both raise your LDL (bad) cholesterol and lower your HDL (good) cholesterol. Typical sources of trans fats include deep-fried fast foods, bakery products, packaged snack foods, margarine, and crackers. Heart-healthy eating isn't all about cutting back, though. Most people, for instance, need to add more fruits and vegetables to their diet, with a goal of 5 to 10 servings a day. "There's a huge amount of data to suggest that fruits and vegetables are highly effective in preventing not just cardiovascular disease, but cancer and other diseases as well," according to doctors at the Mayo Clinic.

Omega-3 fatty acids may decrease your risk of heart attack, protect against irregular heartbeats, and lower blood pressure. Some fish are a good natural source of omega-3s. Omega-3s are present in smaller amounts in flaxseed oil, walnut oil, soybean oil, and canola oil, and they can also be found in supplements.

Following a heart-healthy diet also means drinking alcohol only in moderation—no more than two drinks a day for men, one a day for women. At that moderate level, alcohol can have a protective effect on your heart. Above that, it becomes a health hazard.

Researchers in England find promise in broccoli, which has been found to repair heart damage caused by diabetes by producing an enzyme that protects heart vessels. Previous research has shown broccoli linked to a lower risk of heart attack and stroke. Not many of us like broccoli, but this type of evidence suggests that we should add it to our diet not only as a preventative, but also as a way of developing good heart health if you are diabetic.

4. Maintain a healthy weight

As you put on weight in adulthood, you gain mostly fatty tissue. This excess weight can lead to conditions that increase your chances of heart disease, such as high blood pressure, high cholesterol, and diabetes.

How do you know if your weight is healthy? Waist circumference is a useful tool to assess abdominal fat. In general, men are considered overweight if their waist measurement is greater than 40 inches. And women, in general, are overweight if their waist measurement is greater than 35 inches. Even small reductions in weight can be beneficial. Reducing your weight by just 10 percent can decrease your blood pressure, lower your blood cholesterol level, and reduce your risk of diabetes. Weight loss also lessens pressure on one's knees, back, ankles, and feet, which can prevent considerable discomfort as we age.

5. Get regular health screenings

High blood pressure and high cholesterol can damage your cardiovascular system, including your heart. But without testing for them, you probably won't know whether you have these conditions. Regular screening can tell you what your numbers are and whether you need to take action. Regular blood pressure screenings start in childhood. Adults should have their blood pressure checked at least every two years. You may need more frequent checks if your numbers aren't optimal or if you have other risk factors for cardiovascular disease. Optimal blood pressure is less than 120/80 millimeters of mercury.

Adults should have their cholesterol measured at least once every five years. You may need more frequent testing if your numbers aren't optimal, or if you have other risk factors for cardiovascular disease. Some children may need their blood cholesterol tested if they have a strong family history of heart disease.

6. Aspirin and heart health

A low dose of aspirin (50 mg) appears to be just as effective as a higher dose (325 mg) in preventing a heart attack, stroke or death among patients with stable cardiovascular disease, according to researchers at Duke University Medical Center (2008). In reviewing data from nearly 10,000 patients enrolled in these trials, researchers discovered that those who took aspirin daily had a 25 percent reduction in the risk of stroke, a 26 percent reduction in risk of a second heart attack, and a 13 percent lower risk of death when compared with people who took a placebo. Overall, in considering all types of cardiovascular events, patients who took aspirin were 21 percent less likely to encounter potentially fatal problems than those who did not.

Aspirin helps protect a person from heart attacks because it can break up platelets in the blood. These platelets tend to clump together in clots that can block blood vessels and lead to chest pain or heart attack. To illustrate, the study found that physicians would need to treat only 71 people with low-dose aspirin to prevent a single death, but they would have to treat 83 patients with cholesterol lowering drugs (statins) or 91 patients with blood pressure drugs (ACE-inhibitors) to achieve the same result.

■ Preventing Diabetes

The Centers for Disease Control and Prevention (CDC; 2008) reports that 12.2 million, or 23.1 percent of all people 60 and over, have diabetes. The following data on the impact of the disease comes from a 2008 CDC report.

In 2004, heart disease was noted on 68 percent of diabetes-related death certificates among people aged 65 years or older.

- In 2004, stroke was noted on 16 percent of diabetes-related death certificates among people aged 65 years or older.
- Adults with diabetes have heart disease death rates about two to four times higher than adults without diabetes.
- The risk for stroke is two to four times higher among people with diabetes.
- According to death certificate reports, diabetes contributed to a total of 233,619 deaths in 2005, the latest year for which data on contributing causes of death are available.
- Diabetes is the leading cause of new cases of blindness among adults aged 20–74 years. Diabetic retinopathy causes 12,000 to 24,000 new cases of blindness each year.
- Diabetes is the leading cause of kidney failure, accounting for 44 percent of new cases in 2005.
- About 60 to 70 percent of people with diabetes have mild to severe forms of nervous system damage. The results of such damage include impaired sensation or pain in the feet or hands, slowed digestion of food in the stomach, carpal tunnel syndrome, erectile dysfunction, or other nerve problems.
- Severe forms of diabetic nerve disease are a major contributing cause of lower-extremity amputations.

Although there are many reasons for the high rates of diabetes among older adults, including heredity, pancreatic disease, and cardiovascular problems, the primary reason is obesity coupled with inactivity and a diet high in carbohydrates. Like many of us, a friend of ours began putting on weight in his 50s, although he was still an avid tennis player. He was told by doctors he saw about a higher blood sugar reading for at least five years before he did anything about it. Six months before he was diagnosed with Type 2 (non-insulin dependent diabetes), he said that he was about 60 pounds overweight and not very active. His doctor called to say his three-month average blood sugars (called a Hemoglobin A1C test) were high. How high? 7.8 or an average blood sugar of 170–180. Normal is 100 and below. He said he promised himself that he would lose weight, but that was easier said then done. Five months later, he got violently ill and found out that his blood sugars had risen to 260, a seriously high number. He was placed on a well-known diabetes medication called Metformin and also promptly lost 40 pounds. Within two months, his blood sugars were around 100 fasting in the morning. He returned to tennis, began hiking, and started a diet low in carbohydrates (sugar). He'd still like to lose 20 pounds. It's tough, he told us, since weight loss isn't that easy, but he had his scare and it's had a positive impact on his health. He no longer needs diabetes medication. His waist size has dropped from 44" to 38". He plays two hours of singles tennis against much younger opponents and feels healthier than he has in years. He's stopped drinking alcohol since the thought of it is repugnant to him. Having gone to a diabetes dietitian, he follows her advice and feels content with his diet. It's almost a religious experience, he says, because the discipline has changed his life, including his work habits, and he feels extraordinarily healthy.

Preventing diabetes involves the following:

1. Keeping your weight at its suggested level.
2. Being active every day for an hour.
3. Following a healthy low-fat, low-carbohydrate diet.
4. Not smoking, and drinking only small amounts of alcohol.
5. Keeping stress in check.
6. Having your blood sugars checked periodically. You can buy blood sugar monitors cheaply and check your blood sugars in the morning when you wake up and before dinner. If your readings are above 120, see your doctor. It's a sign that something's wrong.
7. If your blood pressure is high, your waist is over 40" for men and 35" for women, and your cholesterol is high, then you're at very high risk of heart difficulties. Smaller waist size is always considered to be much healthier.

▪ Summary

This chapter discusses maintaining good health before and after retirement. Special attention is paid to common health problems of older adults including heart problems, adult onset diabetes, and the loss of cognitive functioning related to Alzheimer's and other forms of brain disorders. Special attention is given to recognizing problems as they occur and then seeking out appropriate medical care.

▪ Useful Web Sites

Alzheimer's Association. http://www.alz.org/index.asp.
American Heart Association. http://www.americanheart.org/presenter.jhtml?identifier=1200000.
Diabetes Information (American Diabetes Association). http://www.diabetes.org/home.jsp.
Senior Health (Medline Plus). http://www.nlm.nih.gov/medlineplus/senior-shealth.html.

Young at Heart (Government Web site for health tips for older adults). http://www.alz.org/index.asp.

■ References

American Heart Association. 2008. Heart Attack and Angina Statistics. http://www.americanheart.org/presenter.jhtml?identifier=4591.

Carle, A. August 2007. "More than a game: Brain training against dementia." *Nursing Homes* pp. 22–24.

Centers for Disease Control and Prevention. January 16, 2008. Diabetes Fact Sheet. Department of Health and Human Services. http://www.cdc.gov/diabetes/pubs/pdf/ndfs_2007.pdfDiabetes.

Colcombe, S., K. Erickson, P. Scalf, J. Kim, R. Prakash, E. McAuley, et al. 2006. "Aerobic exercise training increases brain volume in aging humans." *Journal of Gerontology: Medical Sciences* 61A:1166–70.

Duke University Medical Center. 2008. "Aspirin in heart attack prevention: How much, how long?" http://www.dukemednews.org/news/article.php?id=10217.

George, L. 2007. "The secret to not losing your marbles." *Macleans*, 36–39.

Lawton, M. P. 1977. "The impact of the environment on aging and behavior." In *Handbook of the Psychology of Aging*, eds. J. E. Birren and K. W. Schaie, 276–301. New York: Van Nostrand Reinhold.

Lunde, A. March 24, 2008. "Preventing Alzheimer's: Exercise still best bet." http://www.mayoclinic.com/health/alzheimers/MY00002.

Mayo Clinic. Preventing Heart Attacks. 2008. http://www.mayoclinic.com/health/heart-attack/DS00094/DSECTION=prevention.

National Institute for Aging. 2008. Alzheimer's Disease Education and Referral Center. Referral Connections 15(4). http://www.nia.nih.gov/Alzheimers/ResearchInformation/Newsletter/CurrentIssue.htm.

Robert, S. A., and L. W. Li. 2001. "Age variation in the relationship between community socioeconomic status and adult health." *Research on Aging* 23(2): 233–58.

Scarmeas, N., Y. Stern, M.-X. Tang, R. Mayeux, and J. Luchsinger. 2006. "Mediterranean Diet and risk of Alzheimer's disease." *Annals of Neurology*. http://www.eurekalert.org/pub_releases/2006-04/jws-mdl041106.php.

Vaillant, G. E., and K. Mukamal, K. 2001. "Successful aging." *American Journal of Psychiatry* 158(6): 839–47.

Wilson, R. S., J. A. Schneider, S. E. Arnold, J. L. Bienias, and D. A. Bennett. October 20, 2007. "Conscientiousness and the incidence of Alzheimer disease and cognitive impairment." *Archives of General Psychiatry* 64: pp. 1204, 1212.

18 ▪ ▪ ▪

Finding Good Medical Care

This chapter is about the most important topic in the book—your health and how to find and properly use good medical care. This is particularly important if you've decided to move to a new community, since you will have to do the sometimes time-consuming and often difficult task of selecting a physician who is not only good, but is someone you can work with. I've gone to some lengths to describe some of the problems with finding new medical care, and also of going to the research literature to alert you to what others say is important to their satisfaction with doctors and hospitals. Granted, someone else's satisfaction may not be the same as yours, but there is comfort in knowing how others view the people and services you will likely use in your new community. Be prepared for how tough it is to find a good doctor who will also agree to accept you as a new patient. As I will point out, we have a doctor shortage in many locations in America that attract retirees.

■ Steps to Finding Good Medical Care

Start locating medical care before you move

As many of you are about to discover, medical care is not always the best or the easiest to come by in new communities. Before moving to Prescott from Los Angeles, one person told us that he called every internist and family physician in Prescott on his supplemental medical insurance list (60 physicians). He found one doctor who would see him, but he was 12 miles from his home. No one else was taking new patients. Right before he moved from Los Angeles, he got violently ill. After a week of not getting better, he called the doctor he had chosen and was told he could see our friend, but not for a month. He ended up going to the local emergency room, where his bill was more than $3,000. He spent the next few weeks again calling every doctor on his insurance list, only to be told that they were not taking new patients or that he couldn't be seen for six months.

The fact is that, like many communities in America that retirees favor, Prescott has half the national average of doctors. With an average age of people in the county around 60, there are too few primary care doctors to handle the needs of the many older patients in the area. There are counties in rural Arizona with only two or three doctors for the entire county, and these counties cover huge geographic areas.

We have a serious primary care doctor shortage in many sections of the country, and our hospitals are not nearly as good as we would like to think they are. Don't let anyone kid you about America having the best medical care in the world. We don't. We just pay more for it. An editorial in the *New York Times* (August 12, 2007) reports that, in an evaluation of health care systems in 191 countries, the United States ranked 37. In the area of fairness, the United States ranked dead last in the disparity of quality care between richer and poorer Americans. Americans with below-average incomes are much less likely than their counterparts in other industrialized nations to see a doctor when sick, to fill prescriptions, or to get needed tests and follow-up care. In an eight-country comparison including England, Australia, and Canada, the United States ranked last in years of potential life lost to circulatory diseases, respiratory diseases, and diabetes, and had the second-highest death rate from bronchitis, asthma, and emphysema.

Our health care problem is serious. As the population ages and more older people need medical care, the doctor shortage and quality issues will grow. Before you move, make sure that if you *do* find someone, he or she will see you in a crisis. Many communities have doctor referral services that will help you contact doctors taking new patients. You can also find doctors taking new patients who advertise in the local paper. Our suggestion is that you call the local hospitals in the area you plan to move to and get the names of those doctors who are taking new patients. Many are new doctors to the area who are building a practice, doctors who have moved from working in a group practice to working alone, and doctors who have had losses in their patient loads. Be sure to find out if the doctor has board certification since this indicates that they have met national requirements in their area of practice.

A new condition of being accepted by a physician is now playing out in many communities. Some doctors are now charging patients an upfront yearly fee to be assured of immediate care and longer appointments. These doctors limit the number of patients they see to assure better care. In the Phoenix area, these doctors are charging patients up to $1,500 a year for what has been dubbed "boutique medical practice."

Bring your medical records with you

It's a very good idea to bring all of your most current medical information with you. This is because doctors often don't send medical information on to new doctors in a timely fashion (or at all). Having a checkup and any other medical care before you leave home is also a good idea since, as we've noted earlier, it takes time to find the right doctor for you. You should also get your former doctor to commit to accepting a telephone call once you've moved if you have a crisis and can't find a new doctor to see you. Good doctors feel a responsibility to get you settled in a new community and will be willing to help out until you are settled.

Fill prescriptions before you move

Fill your prescriptions before you move and make certain your mail order pharmacy, if you use one, has your new address. Not all states accept a prescription from a doctor in another state, particularly if the medication is a controlled substance (sleeping pills or anti-anxiety medications, for example). Finding the best pharmacy to use locally also takes time, and some comparison-shopping may be needed. Some doctors don't fill out prescriptions correctly, and having a supply of your medications will prevent you from going without your medications. Are we being unreasonable? No. We've spoken to a number of people who use diabetes equipment (lancets, strips, etc.) who have told us that pharmacies are very strict about accepting prescriptions because if they are incorrectly written, Medicare won't pay and will even fine the pharmacy if it fills the prescription incorrectly. So have a supply of your medications on hand before you move.

Almost all supplementary Medicare plans cover medication. It is to your advantage to use mail order services, which are much cheaper than going to your local drug store, but also provide generics. One supplementary plan we know of offered through the state of California provides a three-month supply of a generic drug for $10, a drug that is on their formulary for $25, and a non-formulary drug for $75. The cost of filling prescriptions at the pharmacy is much higher. Medco, which is the mail order company currently used by the state of California, provides online ordering, which makes the entire process painless and fast.

Be sure to research the quality of hospital care in a new community

Let's first consider the issue of good medical care and where you can find it. *US News and World Report* (June 4, 2008; http://health.usnews.com/sections/health/best-hospitals) evaluated 5,462 hospitals, but only 173 met a high standard in one or more specialties. Most that did were referral centers, places accustomed to seeing the toughest patients and conducting bench-to-bedside research that advances the state of the art. Of the 173 ranked hospitals, just 18 made the super elite honor roll. These are medical centers that scored at or near the top in a minimum of six specialties. The report says that while local hospitals may do a good job for nonserious problems, the best hospitals do a superb job. Here's the way the report determined the best American hospitals:

Reputation

For each of the 16 specialties, a randomized sample of 200 board-certified specialists was selected from the American Medical Association's master file of more than 850,000 U.S. doctors, and those physicians were mailed a survey form. They were asked to list the five hospitals they think are best in their specialty for difficult cases, without taking location or expense into account (or naming their own hospital).

Mortality Rate

What is more important than a hospital's ability to keep patients alive? The number shown is a ratio—a comparison of the number of deaths of Medicare inpatients with certain conditions that occurred with the number that was expected (after adjusting for severity of condition) during 2003, 2004, and 2005. An index number below 1.00 means the hospital did better than expected and above 1.00 means worse than expected. Deaths were included if they occurred within 30 days from the date of admission, except for cancer, in which only deaths from admission to discharge were included. Severity adjustments were derived from 3M Health Information Systems software (All Patient Refined Diagnosis Related Group).

The report lists the top 50 hospitals for each of several serious medical conditions. The best-ranked treatment center for cancer, the University of Texas M. D. Anderson Cancer Center in Houston, Texas, has a score of 100. Even though it's not close to home, if I could afford it I'd want to go to the best place I could find for cancer treatment. For heart problems, the Cleveland Clinic was ranked number one and is where I'd go if I had a serious heart problem and could afford it.

We looked up my local hospital in Prescott, the Yavapai Regional Hospital, on a United States Health and Human Services Web site called HospitalCompare (http://www.hospitalcompare.hhs.gov/Hospital/Search/Welcome.asp?version=default&browser=IE%7C7%7CWinXP&language=English&defaultstatus=0&pagelist=Home), which gives a great deal of information about local hospitals in the United States treating Medicare patients. We were interested in patient satisfaction with treatment for acute heart care, a very common emergency condition for older adults. The satisfaction ratings were mostly in the 70 percent range, with such things as explanation of medication and treatment after they left, but only 71 percent of the treated patients would recommend the hospital to others.

In another retirement area, Southern California, Desert Regional Medical Center in Palm Springs had higher emergency room deaths than the state average, and in terms of patient satisfaction rated lower on every indicator by as much as 10 points lower than the entire state. Only 60 percent would recommend this hospital to others. In the southern Florida area, costs were fully $2,000 higher for acute heart care than in Phoenix, and patient satisfaction rated from only 51 percent at Mt. Sinai to 77 percent at Baptist Hospital. Kendall Medical Center in Miami had a dismal 42 percent who would recommend the hospital for acute care. In Tucson, another large retirement area, at Tucson Heart Hospital, 83 percent of the patients would recommend the hospital for acute treatment of a heart problem (it's the third highest-rated hospital in Arizona), while only 57 percent of Carondolet St. Josephs Hospital patients would recommend the hospital for similar care. As you can see, hospitals are not created equal, and wise people do their homework for a specific condition before using a hospital.

Is the lack of good medical care a deal breaker should you decide to move after you retire? No, and it depends on how healthy you are when you retire, but it's a consideration. Many people in Prescott complain about the poor medical care and use facilities in Phoenix, about a two-hour drive away. This can be fine if you're not dealing with an emergency, but with a serious life or death situation it could be fatal. Would we not have moved to Prescott had we known about the doctor shortage? Not at all. It's a great place, and there are signs that medical care is improving. The local hospital in Prescott opened a new facility on the east side of the community (about 10 miles from downtown Prescott), which was ranked the second best hospital by patient satisfaction in the state. We think the marketplace has a strong impact on services. The more people complain, and the more they use services outside the community, the more responsive providers often become. You should still be an informed consumer and make inquiries about medical care before you move to a new community.

What to look for in a doctor

Good doctors listen, ask good questions, take their time with you, and want your opinion. Bad doctors have their minds made up about what's wrong with you within 30 seconds of meeting you. This type of error has been written about in medical journals and is said to be one of the most important reasons doctors misdiagnose. Doctors should be patient and not give you a sense that they're in a rush. Patients who feel rushed by doctors usually don't tell them everything they need to know and often leave the hospital unconvinced of the doctor's diagnosis and treatment. How do we know this? Fifty percent of all prescriptions are either not used at all or are not used as labeled (Kane and Glicken, 1977). When you don't trust physicians, you tend not to trust their advice.

Here is some research on patient satisfaction with their medical care that may help you select a physician:

1. A number of studies, including a study by the Ontario Provincial Government, found that patients with lower back pain were more satisfied with chiropractic treatment than with treatment by a medical doctor. Cherkin and MacCormack (1989) found that patients were three times more satisfied with chiropractic care than with care by family physicians. In addition, the patient's perception of the doctor's confidence in diagnosing and treating low back pain was almost three times higher in patients receiving chiropractic care than with those receiving care from family physicians.

2. Studies call into question whether many people with arthritis and meniscus tears in their knees are needlessly undergoing arthroscopic knee surgery. Studies have found that surgery for either problem "probably isn't terribly helpful compared to just medication and physical therapy," said Dr. C. David Geier Jr., a spokesman for the American Orthopaedic Society for Sports Medicine (Associated Press, 2008). The overuse of surgery for both conditions also leads to unnecessary MRIs and other expensive, but unhelpful, diagnostic procedures that may not be covered by many insurance policies.

3. Beach and colleagues (2005) found that patients who reported being treated with dignity and who were involved in their medical decisions were more satisfied and more likely to adhere to their doctor's recommendations.

4. Gross, Zyzanski, Borawski, Cebul, and Stange (1998) found that the amount of time a physician spends with a patient plays an important role in patient satisfaction, with satisfaction rates improving as visit length increases. Time spent chatting during the visit was also related to higher rates of satisfaction. Zyzanski and colleagues (1998) found that physicians with high-volume practices were more efficient with their time, but had lower rates of patient satisfaction, offered

fewer preventive services, and were viewed as less sensitive in the doctor-patient relationship.

5. Shaw and colleagues (2005) found that doctor-patient communication affects patient satisfaction. When patients who went to their family physicians for low back pain felt that communication with the physician was positive (i.e., the physician took the problem seriously, explained the condition clearly, tried to understand the patient's job, and gave advice to prevent reinjury), their rates of satisfaction were higher than could be explained by just feeling better.

6. Cecil and Killeen (1997) found that when physicians encourage patients to express their ideas, concerns, and expectations, patients were more satisfied with their visits and more likely to follow the physician's advice.

7. Rao and colleagues (2000) found that when physicians recognize and address patient expectations, satisfaction is higher not only for the patient, but also for the physician. The researchers found that about 10 percent of patients failed to tell the physician about a service or referral they wanted because the physician seemed disinterested.

8. Finally, Otani and colleagues (2005) found that a physician's ability to make the correct diagnosis and craft an effective treatment plan were more important than his or her "bedside manner," although this finding is offset by other findings that suggest bedside manner is very important. Obviously, competence coupled with good bedside manner make patients the most satisfied.

Be your own advocate

Because the Internet provides so much medical information, you no longer have to take your doctor's word for the best treatment for a condition. You have access to a wealth of information through sites like Webmd.com, Mayoclinic.com, Americanheart.org, American Psychological Association (Apa.com), and a number of other useful Web sites that provide easy-to-read information about medical conditions, medication, and almost anything else you would want to know about a doctor's diagnosis and treatment. If you need surgery, many of the Web sites have videos of the surgery and information you might not get from the surgeon. We have a list of good Web sites to consult about medical problems at the end of the chapter. We urge you to read about the conditions your doctor diagnoses and to be certain the diagnosis is correct before taking medication you may not need or that may do harm. Not all doctors appreciate the time and effort you spend looking for information online. That's their problem. A good physician welcomes a knowledgeable patient.

Don't get x-rays or extensive tests unless you're certain you need them

Mishori (2008) notes that some researchers worry about overexposure to radiation and estimate that "1% to 2% more cases of cancer may result from the increased use of imaging in the future." Imaging may also result in "false-positive" results (finding a problem that does not in fact exist) or "incidental findings" (seeing an abnormality that may be clinically harmless). Both results often lead to even more imaging and risky invasive procedures, including surgery. Although CT scans (also known as CAT scans) are particularly good for looking at organs, bone, soft tissue, and blood vessels, their radiation is typically the equivalent of about one hundred conventional x-rays.

Mishori (2008) notes that typical problems in which imaging is overused, such as back pain, usually go away on their own within six to eight weeks, and most back problems do not need x-rays, MRIs, or CT scans. Imaging should be reserved for those cases in which pain does not go away and a serious underlying condition is suspected.

Why then are so many x-rays and excessive tests done that are probably unnecessary? Mishori (2008) gives the following reasons:

- **Short appointment times.** With less time available to spend with patients, some doctors may order images as a shortcut—a way to get quick answers.
- **Malpractice fears.** Excessive litigation forces doctors to practice defensive medicine. Even if there is little chance of a serious disease or condition, a physician may order a test to reduce the risk of being sued later for missing something important.
- **Where the money is.** A growing number of physicians own diagnostic facilities or equipment. Some may have an incentive to order tests because the fee goes to their own bottom line.
- **Patient expectations.** Many patients want what they consider "the best"—sophisticated technologies like CT scans or MRIs—and doctors are quick to comply even if they don't really see the need.
- **Patient reassurance.** Sometimes, all evidence aside, it is easier to lower a patient's anxiety by pointing to an actual CT image and saying, "See, there is no tumor there." In some cases, a picture may be worth 1,000 words (or dollars).

Before getting any test that may not be necessary or could cause harm, be sure and ask the following: (a) Do I really need it? Learn about the various tests and what each is best for. Then talk with your doctor about the risks involved, such as radiation and false-positive results. (b) Why is a specific imaging test necessary? How certain are you about the diagnosis without the scan? A medical history and physical may be enough for a diagnosis and treatment plan. (c) How will test results affect treatment decisions? Does another, safer, test exist that would give me the same information? (d) If you do have a CT scan or an MRI, be sure to obtain a copy with the report on a CD-ROM. This will save you the trouble of repeating the imaging.

Know about your insurance

At age 65, if you are Social Security eligible by having contributed to Social Security for at least 40 quarters, you can and should sign up for Medicare at your local Social Security office three to five months before your 65th birthday. Medicare Part A covers major medical expenses, including hospital care and rehabilitation for a time-limited period. It is free if you sign up before your 65th birthday and are eligible, but it carries a $1,040.00 deductible. To offset what Medicare doesn't cover, Medicare Part B covers a variety of medical treatments not covered or not fully covered by Medicare Part A. Currently anyone who is single and making $82,000 a year or less pays $96.40 per month for Medicare Part B. Those who are single or married, but make up to $164,000, pay higher premiums, which change periodically. There is a $135 deductible each year before Medicare kicks in for Part B.

Estimates are that you should budget between $5,500 and $7,500 a year after age 65 to cover expenses not covered by Medicare Parts A and B, or $225,000 over a normal post-65 lifetime (Andrews, 2008). A couple without employer-sponsored retiree coverage can expect to need anywhere from $194,000 to $635,000 to cover health care premiums and out-of-pocket costs during retirement (Andrews, 2008), which includes premiums, deductibles, items not covered by Medicare, and medication. Currently, medication is not fully covered until you've paid $4,500 out of pocket. Even with very good supplementary plans, those of you on blood pressure, diabetes, and other medications normal for many older adults can easily pay $1,000–$2,000 out of pocket each year. Don't make the mistake that many retiring people make who think Medicare pays for all medical expenses (it doesn't), or that your current medical plan with an employer will extend into retirement. For many of you it won't.

Medicare and supplementary insurance are complicated issues for most older adults. Medicare is very good at explaining its benefits. You can call or visit your local Social Security office to have Medicare and supplemental coverage explained. Be aware of several issues; there has been a good deal of difficulty with some insurance companies offering supplemental plans telling insured older adults that they have coverage they don't really have. Some plans have a less-than-positive track record for timely payment of bills. The government has rules about what policies have to include, but has been lax in enforcing those rules. Companies you can trust, like AARP, which offers supplementary coverage, are ones you should consider. Another issue is that Medicare is running out of money. We have no doubt but that premiums will increase and some coverage will decrease as a result. Patterson (2008) notes some of these problems:

> The supply of primary care physicians is drying up. Medical students, viewing the declining income and high-hassle lifestyles of primary care docs, are flocking to specialty training. Primary care physicians are not being produced at replacement rates. We don't like to think about it, but Medicare Part A has an unfunded liability over the next 75 years of $11.6 trillion. That means if we don't do anything, don't add new benefits, don't include new beneficiary groups, don't raise or lower any taxes, there will be an $11.6 trillion gap between the cost of hospital services we promised to people already alive and money available to pay for it. That doesn't include Medicare payments to health-care providers (Part B) or the Medicare drug benefit (Part D). It doesn't account for Medicaid, Social Security or other entitlements. All told, we're handing off a $50 trillion to $60 trillion obligation to future generations with no means of meeting it. (p. 1)

How serious is the problem? A study done at Harvard University (Hollmer, 2008) says that only 5 percent of graduating doctors plan to go into primary care. The reason, they believe, is that Medicare severely limits the salaries of primary care doctors because of its reimbursement system, which does not compensate primary care doctors for phone calls they make to you, contacts with specialists on your behalf, or a number of important services. The result is that the average primary care doctor makes $165,000 a year for often putting in a 60-hour week, while the average hematologist makes more than $500,000 a year. Changing the reimbursement system might mean that specialists receive less money from Medicare, and will likely not accept Medicare patients, a disaster for most retirees. What can you do? Be very active in the Medicare debate and let your legislators know what you think. And be aware of the need to have very good secondary insurance, which might provide better coverage should Medicare reduce benefits. Almost everyone we read believes that Medicare will reduce benefits, leaving a larger share of the bill to older adults. Plan for higher medical expenses. It seems inevitable to us.

The government allows 12 supplementary plans, each with a different premium, deductible, and coverage. Some offer long-term nursing home care but are expensive, while others offer very basic care, have small deductibles and co-pays, and are generally affordable but have few frills. We've included several Web sites at the end of the chapter to help better explain Medicare Parts A and B, and now with medications covered under all plans, Part D. Keep in mind that your supplementary insurance plan determines which medical providers will be reimbursed at full coverage. You'll need to check with your supplementary plan to determine if doctors, hospitals, and other providers are covered, and if not, what the out-of-pocket expense will be to you. It's a very good idea to determine which supplementary plan you will choose based on the number of medical providers included in the plan in a community and geographic area.

Each of the 12 supplementary plans (A–L) approved by the government is required to have specific coverage, but the cost for each plan differs by where you live and the insurance company you choose. A review of the cost for each plan suggests the need to shop around for the best price and coverage. We looked at programs in two states and found wide differences in the cost of plans providing the same benefits. In California, for example, Plan F cost $1,334 with Mutual of Omaha, while Standard Life and Accident Company charged $2,190 for the same plan, a 64 percent difference in cost. In Texas, the same plan ranged from $1,466 for Constitution Life to $3,589 with Oxford Life Insurance, a 144 percent difference (O'Rourke, 2008). You need to consider price, but also concerns about the company you choose and whether it has a good reputation for paying benefits in a timely manner. Plans change frequently.

■ Summary

This chapter discusses the growing body of information on how to live a healthy older adult life. Health issues that include heart problems, diabetes, and Alzheimer's are discussed along with an explanation of insurance plans, Medicare, and Supplemental Medicare Insurance. Special attention is given to choosing physicians, having medical information handy, and the growing difficulty of finding good medical care should you move to a new community. The chapter also discusses research suggesting that many routine procedures done on older adults are not only unnecessary, but may also cause more harm than good.

■ Useful Web Sites

American Psychiatric Association. Information about medical treatment of emotional problems. http://www.psych.org.
American Psychological Association. Information about common emotional problems. http://www.apa.org.
Mayo Clinic: More than 800 Diseases and Conditions. http://www.mayoclinic.com/health/DiseasesIndex/DiseasesIndex.
Medicare booklet outlining everything you'll need to know about Medicare and supplementary Insurance. http://www.medicare.gov/Publications/Pubs/pdf/10050.pdf.
Medigap. Information about supplementary insurance. http://www.medicareadvocacy.org/faq_medigap.htm.
RxList. A Web site providing information on more than 200 medications. http://www.rxlist.com/script/main/hp.asp.
WebMD. Gives information about 800 medical conditions, treatments, and medications. http://www.webmd.com.

■ References

Andrews, M. "Costs After 65: Ouch, Even With Medicare." *US News and World Report,* June 4, 2008, http://www.usnews.com/blogs/on-health-and-money/2008/6/4/health-costs-after-65-ouch-even-with-medicare.html.

Associated Press. "Arthroscopic knee surgery no help for many." http://www.msnbc.msn.com/id/26644064 (accessed October 7, 2008).

Beach, M. C., J. Sugarman, R. L. Johnson, J. J. Arbelaez, P. S. Duggan, and L. A. Cooper. 2005. "Do patients treated with dignity report higher satisfaction, adherence and receipt of preventive care?" *Annals of Family Medicine.* 3:331–38.

Cecil, D. W., and I. Killeen. 1997. "Control, compliance and satisfaction in the family practice encounter." *Family Medicine* 29: 653–57.

Cherkin, D., and F. MacCormack. 1989. "Patient evaluations of care from family physicians and chiropractors." *Western Journal of Medicine* 150:351–55.

Gross, D. A., S. J. Zyzanski, E. A. Borawski, R. D. Cebul, and K. D. Stange. 1998. "Patient satisfaction with time spent with their physician." *Journal of Family Practice* 47: 33–37.

Hollmer, M. "Harvard researchers say Medicare worsens primary care doctor shortage." *Boston Business Journal,* July 7, 2008, http://www.bizjournals.com/boston/stories/2008/07/07/daily9.html.

Kane, R., and M. D. Glicken. 1977. Compliance and Consumerism: Complementary Goals of Social Work in Health Settings (with Rosalee Kane). Presented to the National Symposium of the National Association of Social Workers, San Diego, California, November 1977.

Mishori, R. "The danger of too many tests." *Parade Magazine.* July 6, 2008. http://www.parade.com/articles/editions/2008/edition_07-06-2008/3Too_Many_Tests.

New York Times. August 12, 2007. "World's Best Medical Care?" http://www.nytimes.com/2007/08/12/opinion/12sun1.html?th=&emc=th&pagewanted= print.

O'Rourke, D. O. 2008. "Maneuvering Medigap." The street.com. http://www.thestreet.com/story/10308239/1/thestreetcom-ratings-maneuvering-medigap.html (accessed August 18, 2008).

Otani, K., R. S. Kurz, and L. E. Harris. 2005. "Managing primary care using patient satisfaction measures." *Journal of Healthcare Management* 50:311–24.

Patterson, T. C. "Medicare's future: Our unspoken problem." *East Valley Tribune,* January 14, 2008, http://www.goldwaterinstitute.org/AboutUs/ArticleView.aspx?id=1974.

Rao, J. K., M. Weinberger, and K. Kroenke. 2000. "Visit-specific expectations and patient-centered outcomes: A literature review." *Archives of Family Medicine* 9:1148–55.

Shaw, W. S., A. Zaia, G. Pransky, T. Winters, and W. B. Patterson. 2005. "Perceptions of provider communication and patient satisfaction for treatment of acute low back pain." *Journal of Occupational Environmental Medicine* 47:1036–43.

U.S. Department of Health & Human Services. HospitalCompare. http://www.hospitalcompare.hhs.gov/Hospital/Search/Welcome.asp?version=default&browser=IE%7C7%7CWinXP&language=English&defaultstatus=0&pagelist=Home.

Zyzanski, D. J., K. D. Stange, D. Langa, and S. A. Flocke. 1998. "Trade-offs in high-volume primary care practice." *Journal of Family Practice* 46:397–402.

19 ▪ ▪ ▪

Older Adults Who Abuse Alcohol and Drugs

One of the most common problems facing older adults in retirement is substance abuse, which can take the form of alcohol abuse, legal prescription drug abuse, and illegal drug usage. Often these problems predate retirement, but in some cases they begin to develop after retirement. Because of health problems that result from substance abuse, it is very important that you recognize either actual or potential problems with substance abuse before retirement and do something definite about it. This chapter describes the conditions under which substance abuse is considered a health problem, the treatment used with moderate substance abuse problems in older adults, and a case example of an older adult woman abusing substances after retirement.

▪ The Prevalence of Substance Abuse in Older Adults

Because older adults sometimes experience loneliness and feelings of isolation, alcohol and prescription drug abuse among adults 60 and older is one of the fastest-growing health problems facing the country. Blow (2007) believes that "even as the number of older adults suffering from these disorders climbs, the situation remains underestimated, under-identified, under-diagnosed, and under-treated" (p. 1). Blow reports that substance abuse often has a serious impact on the health of older adults and writes:

> The reality is that misuse and abuse of alcohol and other drugs take a greater toll on affected older adults than on younger adults. In addition to the psychosocial issues that are unique to older adults, aging also ushers in biomedical changes that influence the effects that alcohol and drugs have on the body. Alcohol abuse, for example, may accelerate the normal decline in physiological functioning that occurs with age. In addition, alcohol may elevate older adults' already high risk for injury, illness, and socioeconomic decline. (p. 2)

There are two widely held myths regarding alcohol use among older adults: (a) that it is an infrequent problem; and (b) that when older adults have drinking problems, treatment success is limited. In fact, according to the government, "alcohol abuse among older adults is one of the fastest-growing health problems facing this country (Substance Abuse and Mental Health Services Administration [SAMHSA], 1998) and even a one-time brief encounter of 15 min. or less can reduce nondependent problem drinking by more than 20% (SAMHSA)" (p. 454).

According to the National Institute for Alcohol Abuse and Alcoholism (NIAAA, 1997), roughly 49 percent of all adults aged 60 years and older drink alcohol. Among those aged 60–64 responding to the national survey on drug use and health sponsored by SAMHSA (2004), 50 percent used alcohol in the past month, and 35 percent of individuals aged 65 or older used alcohol in the past month. Of adults aged 65 or older, 6.9 percent reported binge drinking and 1.8 percent reported heavy drinking. Binge drinking is defined as five or more drinks on the same occasion on at least one day in the past month. Heavy drinking is defined as five or more drinks on the same occasion on each of five or more days in the past 30 days. Adams, Barry and Fleming (1996) report that among community-dwelling, noninstitutionalized older adults, two to 15 percent have been shown to exhibit symptoms consistent with alcoholism.

Although the data on older adult alcohol abuse suggests a growing problem, it's difficult to pinpoint alcohol abuse in this population. Even though one-third of all heavy drinkers begin their patterns of alcohol abuse after age 60 (Barrick and Connors, 2002), many symptoms of problem drinking "mimic" physical problems common to this age group, including depression and dementia. Because of stereotypes of older adults by health care professionals, doctors are often unlikely to screen for alcohol problems, particularly in women and older adults who are well educated or affluent. Because alcohol abuse is still considered a morally offensive problem, older adults with substance abuse problems may feel "ashamed" to discuss the problem with their physicians. And because of stereotypes that older adults want to be left alone or have few opportunities for happiness, some health and mental health professionals believe that drinking is one of the few pleasures left to older men and women.

There are a number of serious health consequences of older adult problem drinking. Oslin (2004) reports that even small to moderate amounts of alcohol can increase the risk of hypertension, sleep problems, and malnutrition. The risk of losing one's balance and falling increases with alcohol consumption and significantly increases when 14 or more drinks are consumed per week (Mukamal et al., 2004). Older adults are vulnerable to the negative effects of alcohol because they take more medications than younger people and are therefore at risk for drug or alcohol interactions. Because of slower metabolic and clearance mechanisms, older adults are also more likely to experience adverse drug and alcohol interactions. Slower metabolic and clearance mechanisms delay their resolution. Onder and colleagues (2002) studied alcohol consumption among a population of older adults aged 65–80 and found that even moderate consumption of alcohol increased the risk of an adverse drug reaction by 24 percent.

▧ Related Medical Problems

Stewart and Richards (2000) conclude that a number of older adult medical problems may have their origins in heavy alcohol and drug use. Head injuries and spinal separations as a result of accidents may have been caused by substance abuse. Because heavy drinkers often fail to eat, they may have nutritional deficiencies, which result in psychotic-like symptoms including abnormal eye movements, disorganization, and forgetfulness. Stomach disorders, liver damage, and severe heartburn may have their origins in heavy drinking because alcohol destroys the stomach's mucosal lining. Fifteen percent of all heavy drinkers develop cirrhosis of the liver, and many develop pancreatitis. Weight loss, pneumonia, muscle loss because of malnutrition, and oral cancer have all been associated with heavy drinking. Stewart and Richards (2000) indicate that substance abusers are poor candidates for surgery. Anesthesia and pain medication can delay alcohol withdrawal for up to five days postoperatively. "Withdrawal symptoms can cause agitation and uncooperativeness and can mask signs and symptoms of other postoperative complications. Patients who abuse alcohol are at a higher risk for postoperative complications such as excessive bleeding, infection, heart failure, and pneumonia" (Stewart and Richards, 2000, p. 58).

▧ How to Determine if You or a Loved One Has a Substance Abuse Problem

The diagnostic manual used to determine whether people have emotional problems called the DSM-IV (APA, 1994) uses the following indicators to determine whether substance use is abusive: An overuse of substances causing impairment or distress within a twelve-month period as determined by one of the following: (a) Frequent use of substances that interfere with functioning and the fulfillment of responsibilities at home, work, school, etc.; (b) use of substances that impair functioning in dangerous situations such as driving or the use of machines; (c) use of substances that may lead to arrest for unlawful behaviors; and (d) substance use that seriously interferes with relations, marriage, child-rearing and other interpersonal responsibilities (p. 182). Substance abuse may also lead to slurred speech, lack of coordination, unsteady gait, memory loss, fatigue and depression, feelings of euphoria, and lack of social inhibitions (p. 197).

Short tests

Miller (2001) reports that two simple questions asked to substance abusers have an 80 percent chance of diagnosing substance abuse: "In the past year, have you ever drunk or used drugs more than you meant to?" and, "Have you felt you wanted or needed to cut down on your drinking or drug abuse in the past year?" Miller reports that this simple approach has been found to be an effective diagnostic tool in three controlled studies using random samples and laboratory tests for alcohol and drugs in the blood stream following interviews.

Stewart and Richards (2000) and Bisson, Nadeau, and Demers (1999) suggest that four questions from the CAGE questionnaire are predictive of alcohol abuse. CAGE is an acronym for Cut, Annoyed, Guilty, and Eye-opener (see the following questions). Since many people deny their alcoholism, asking questions in an open, direct, and nonjudgmental way may elicit the best results. The four questions are:

1. **Cut**: Have you ever felt you should cut down on your drinking?
2. **Annoyed**: Have people annoyed you by criticizing your drinking?
3. **Guilty**: Have you ever felt guilty about your drinking?
4. **Eye-opener**: Have you ever had a drink first thing in the morning (eye-opener) to steady your nerves or get rid of a hangover? (Bisson, Nadeau, and Demers, 1999, p. 717)

Stewart and Richards (2000) write, "A patient who answers yes to two or more of these questions probably abuses alcohol; a patient who answers yes to one question should be screened further" (p. 56). Should you ever be stopped by a police officer and asked to take a test to measure alcohol in the bloodstream, Stewart and Richards (2000, p. 59) provide the following blood alcohol levels as measures of the impact of alcohol:

- 0.05% (equivalent to one or two drinks in an average-sized person)—impaired judgment, reduced alertness, loss of inhibitions, euphoria.

- 0.10%—slower reaction times, decreased caution in risk-taking behavior, impaired fine-motor control. Legal evidence of intoxication in most states starts at 0.10%.
- 0.15%—significant and consistent losses in reaction times.
- 0.20%—function of entire motor area of brain measurably depressed, causing staggering. The individual may be easily angered or emotional.
- 0.25%—severe sensory and motor impairment.
- 0.30%—confusion, stupor.
- 0.35%—surgical anesthesia.
- 0.40%—respiratory depression, lethal in about half of the population.
- 0.50%—death from respiratory depression. (p. 59)

■ Understanding the Treatments for Substance Abuse

Short-term treatment

Herman (2000) believes that individual psychotherapy can be helpful in treating substance abusers and suggests five situations in which therapy would be indicated: (a) As an appropriate introduction to treatment; (b) as a way of helping mildly or moderately dependent drug abusers; (c) when there are clear signs of emotional problems such as severe depression, since these problems will interfere with the substance abuse treatment; (d) when clients progressing in 12-step programs begin to experience emerging feelings of guilt, shame, and grief; and (e) when a client's disturbed interpersonal functioning continues after a long period of sustained abstinence and therapy might help prevent a relapse.

One of the most frequently discussed treatment approaches to addiction in the literature is brief counseling. Bien and colleagues (1993) reviewed 32 studies of brief interventions with alcohol abusers and found that, on average, brief counseling reduced alcohol use by 30 percent. However, in a study of brief intervention with alcohol abusers, Chang and colleagues (1999) found that both the treatment and control groups significantly reduced their alcohol use. The difference between the two groups in the reduction of their alcohol abuse was minimal. In a study of 175 Mexican Americans who were abusing alcohol, Burge and colleagues (1997) report that treated and untreated groups improved significantly over time, raising questions about the efficacy of treatment versus natural recovery. In an evaluation of a larger report by *Consumer Reports* on the effectiveness of psychotherapy, Seligman (1995) notes that, "Alcoholics Anonymous (AA) did especially well ... significantly bettering mental health professionals [in the treatment of alcohol and drug-related problems]" (p. 10).

Bien and colleagues (1993) found that two or three 10–15 minute counseling sessions are often as effective as more extensive interventions with older alcohol abusers. The sessions include motivation-for-change strategies, education, assessment of the severity of the problem, direct feedback, contracting and goal setting, behavioral modification techniques, and the use of written materials such as self-help manuals. Brief interventions have been shown to be effective in reducing alcohol consumption, binge drinking, and the frequency of excessive drinking in problem drinkers, according to Fleming and colleagues (1997). Completion rates using brief interventions are better for elder-specific alcohol programs than for mixed-age programs (Atkinson, 1995), and late-onset alcoholics are more likely to complete treatment and have somewhat better outcomes using brief interventions (Liberto and Oslin, 1995).

Miller and Sanchez (1994) summarize the key components of brief substance-abuse counseling using the acronym FRAMES: feedback, responsibility, advice, menu of strategies, empathy, and self-efficacy.

1. **Feedback**: Includes an assessment with feedback to the client regarding the client's risk for alcohol problems, his or her reasons for drinking, the role of alcohol in the patient's life, and the consequences of drinking.
2. **Responsibility**: Includes strategies to help clients understand the need to remain healthy, independent, and financially secure. This is particularly important when working with older clients and clients with health problems and disabilities.
3. **Advice**: Includes direct feedback and suggestions to clients to help them cope with their drinking problems and with other life situations that may contribute to alcohol abuse.
4. **Menu**: Includes a list of strategies to reduce drinking and help cope with such high-risk situations as loneliness, boredom, family problems, and lack of social opportunities.
5. **Empathy**: Bien and colleagues (1993) strongly emphasize the need for a warm, empathetic, and understanding style of treatment. Miller and Rollnick (1991) found that an empathetic counseling style produced a 77 percent reduction in client drinking as compared to a 55 percent reduction when a confrontational approach was used.
6. **Self-efficacy**: This includes strategies to help clients rely on their inner resources to make changes in their drinking behavior. Inner resources may include positive points of view about themselves, helping others, staying busy, and good problem-solving coping skills.

Some additional aspects of brief interventions suggested by Menninger (2002) include drinking agreements in the form of agreed-upon drinking limits that are signed by the patient and the practitioner, ongoing follow-up and support, and appropriate timing of the intervention with the patient's readiness to change. Completion rates for elder-specific alcohol treatment programs are modestly better than for mixed-age programs (Atkinson, 1995). Late-onset alcoholics are also more likely to complete treatment and have somewhat better outcomes (Liberto and Oslin, 1995). Alcoholics Anonymous may be helpful, particularly AA groups that are specifically oriented toward the elderly.

Babor and Higgins-Biddle (2000) discuss the use of brief interventions with people involved in "risky drinking" who are not as yet classified as alcohol dependent. Brief interventions are usually limited to three to five sessions of counseling and education. The intent of brief interventions is to prevent the onset of more serious alcohol-related problems. According to Babor and Higgins-Biddle (2000), "[m]ost programs are instructional and motivational, designed to address the specific behavior of drinking with information, feedback, health education, skill-building, and practical advice, rather than with psychotherapy or other specialized treatment techniques" (p. 676). Higgins-Biddle and colleagues (1997) analyzed 14 random studies of brief interventions that included more than 20,000 risky drinkers. They report a net reduction in drinking of 21 percent for males and 8 percent for females.

Fleming and Manwell (1998) report that people with alcohol-related problems often receive counseling from primary care physicians or nursing staff in five or fewer standard office visits. The counseling consists of rational information about the negative impact of alcohol use, as well as practical advice regarding ways of reducing alcohol dependence and the availability of community resources. Gentilello and colleagues (1995) report that 25–40 percent of the trauma patients seen in emergency rooms may be alcohol dependent. The authors found that a single motivational interview, at or near the time of discharge, reduced drinking levels and re-admission for trauma during six months of follow-up.

Recovery without counseling

Granfield and Cloud (1996) estimate that as many as 90 percent of all problem drinkers never enter treatment and that many end their abuse of alcohol without any form of treatment (Hingson, Scotch, Day, and Culbert, 1980; Roizen, Calahan, Lambert, Wiebel, and Shanks, 1978; Stall and Biernacki, 1989). Sobell, Sobell, Toneatto, and Leo (1993) report that 82 percent of the alcoholics they studied who terminated their addiction did so by using natural recovery methods that excluded the use of professional treatment. As an example of the use of natural recovery techniques, Granfield and Cloud (1996) report that most ex-smokers discontinued their tobacco use without treatment (Peele 1989), while many addicted substance abusers "mature-out" of a variety of addictions including heavy drinking and narcotic use (Snow, 1973; Winick, 1962). Biernacki (1986) reports that people who use natural methods to end their drug addictions utilize a range of strategies, including discontinuing their relationships with drug users, avoiding drug-using environments (Stall and Biernacki 1989), having new goals and interests in their lives (Peele, 1989), and using friends and family to provide a support network (Biernacki, 1986). Trice and Roman (1970) indicate that self-help groups with substance abusing clients are particularly helpful because they develop and continue a support network that assists clients in maintaining abstinence and other changed behaviors.

Granfield and Cloud (1996) studied middle-class alcoholics who used natural recovery alone without professional help or the use of self-help groups. Many of the participants in their study felt that some self-help groups were overly religious, while others believed in alcoholism as a disease that suggested a lifetime struggle. The subjects in the study believed that some self-help groups encouraged dependence on the group and that associating with other alcoholics would probably complicate recovery. In summarizing their findings, Granfield and Cloud (1996) report that:

> Many [research subjects] expressed strong opposition to the suggestion that they were powerless over their addictions. Such an ideology, they explained, not only was counterproductive but was also extremely demeaning. These respondents saw themselves as efficacious people who often prided themselves on their past accomplishments. They viewed themselves as being individualists and strong-willed. One respondent, for instance, explained that "such programs encourage powerlessness" and that she would rather "trust her own instincts than the instincts of others." (p. 51)

Waldorf, Reinarman, and Murphy (1991) found that many addicted people with jobs, strong family ties, and other close emotional supports were able to "walk away" from their very heavy use of cocaine. Granfield and Cloud (1996) note that many of the respondents in their study had a great deal to lose if they continued their substance abuse, and that their sample consisted of people with stable lives, good jobs, supportive families and friends, college educations, and other social supports that gave them motivation to "alter" their drug-using behaviors.

Self-help groups

Humphreys (1998) studied the effectiveness of self-help groups with substance abusers by comparing two groups: one receiving in-patient care for substance abuse, and the other attending self-help groups for substance abuse. At the conclusion of the study, the average participant assigned to a self-help group (AA) had used $8,840 in alcohol-related health care resources as compared to $10,040 for the inpatient treatment participants. In a follow-up study, Humphreys (1998) compared outpatient services to self-help groups for the treatment of substance abuse. The clients in the self-help group had decreased alcohol consumption by 70 percent over three years and consumed 45 percent less health care services (about $1,800 less per person). Humphreys argues that:

> [F]rom a cost-conscious point of view, self-help groups should be the first option evaluated when an addicted individual makes initial contact with professional services (e.g., in a primary care appointment or a clinical assessment at a substance abuse agency or employee assistance program). (1998, p. 16)

▓ A Retired Single Woman Confronts Her Alcoholism

Wanda Anderson is a 69-year-old single woman who lives in an upscale retirement community in Arizona. Wanda was a successful real estate agent in St. Louis for many years and decided to sell her home at the height of the real estate boom and buy a nice home in a retirement community. Wanda moved to her new home in January, 2006, and was ecstatic to find 70-degree weather and many activities in which she could not participate in St. Louis during the winter. However, her first summer in Arizona was a shock, with temperatures hovering in the 100–115 degree range for almost six months without stop. During the hot months, Wanda found that many people left for cooler climates and that her fantasy of many close friends to accompany her on "adventures" evaporated. She was alone and there were few people with whom she could socialize. The community had a bar with a happy hour where cheap drinks and food were available, and Wanda began going every afternoon around 4:00 P.M. and staying increasingly later.

Wanda had never been much of a drinker, but after going to happy hour almost every day for a year, she found that thinking about having a drink gave her great joy. She couldn't wait until 4:00 P.M. to begin. The bar was only a short distance from her home, and she either walked or drove her electric golf cart. One night, driving home from the bar in her cart about 11:00 P.M. when most people were asleep, Wanda missed a turn and her cart went down a steep embankment. She and a friend were to go walking at 6:00 A.M. the next morning before the summer heat became unbearable. Not finding Wanda at home, the friend contacted security and, after a long search, they found Wanda unconscious at the bottom of the embankment with the cart lying partially on top of her.

Wanda was rushed to the hospital, and, thankfully, her injuries were limited to a broken arm and a number of cuts and bruises. More serious was the fact that her blood pressure and blood sugars were extremely high.

Wondering about the possibility of alcohol abuse, the attending physician checked her alcohol level and, even after many hours without alcohol, found it high. He also found evidence of the onset of liver damage and possible heart problems.

When Wanda was awake, the doctor and a social worker interviewed her about her accident and her alcohol consumption. At first she was very defensive, but after a few minutes of avoiding their questions, she admitted that she drank 10–15 drinks, usually martinis, every day at the bar and had even begun having a few drinks before happy hour. A social worker and nurse met with Wanda three additional times over the course of a three-day hospital stay. They gave her information about the health impact of drinking and performed a screening test to determine Wanda's level of abusive drinking. They concluded that she was at very high risk of becoming an alcoholic, since her drinking impaired her judgment and was thought to be responsible for high blood pressure and high blood sugar readings consistent with adult-onset diabetes.

A history taken by the social worker revealed that Wanda was painfully lonely and that the drinking seemed to be a response to early retirement without a plan for what she would do with herself after a lifetime of hard, successful work. The history also revealed that Wanda had come from a family of alcoholics, had vowed to keep her drinking limited, but now realized she was romanticizing alcohol the same way many members of her family had. Wanda had her driver's license revoked, and her ability to drive her golf cart in the retirement community grounds was curtailed to daylight hours and only if someone was with her. She was told by the retirement community CEO that the bylaws of the community required her to go for counseling, and that she had to maintain sobriety for six months before she could have full use of her cart privileges. She was also banned from the bars in the retirement community.

Wanda met with her substance abuse counselor and for the first few sessions was very angry and could only talk about the "hoity-toity" CEO and who did he think he was? She'd seen lots of men like him, and she would just like to tell him a thing or two. But in the third session, Wanda broke down and cried, telling the counselor she made a mistake retiring and leaving her support network in St. Louis. Little did she know, she told the counselor, that she had an aversion to "old people" and hated it here in the community. She thought she'd meet a man, but most of the men were either "jerks, and the same Casanovas she'd been meeting most of her life" or too old and sick to be any fun. She'd spent her first 18 years taking care of "drunks," and she never wanted to take care of anyone again. Still, she was lonely, and loneliness, she admitted, was everything it was cracked up to be.

The first item on the agenda was to focus on resolving the alcohol problem and the issues that seemed to bring about the late-life drinking problem. After some discussion, Wanda pointed out that she didn't like the words *alcoholic* or *drunk* since they were words used to describe members of her family. She did agree that she was drinking too much and that the drinking had health and mental health implications. The social worker asked that Wanda do what she had done so often in her lifetime, and that was to take control of her problem by assertively looking for more information that she could use in counseling. Wanda agreed, and the worker gave her a list of articles on the Internet that she might read for the next session and encouraged Wanda to do her own reading about late-life drinking problems, loneliness, and early retirement.

From the reading of articles suggested by the social worker, they agreed that Wanda had a number of problems that should be dealt with, including feelings of loneliness, lack of work to keep her occupied, little ability to handle leisure time, and alcohol abuse. Wanda brought up the issue of understanding the impact that her alcoholic family had on her current situation.

After months of treatment, during which Wanda would often avoid answering questions directly or would go off on tangents, she began to talk about her feelings and admitted that she has continued drinking heavily. She also drives, although her license has been suspended. She feels strong when she drinks, and loves the peaceful feeling that comes over her as she gets drunk. Like her parents, she romanticizes her drinking and can hardly wait to have her first drink of the day. Sometimes she drinks when she wakes up and often drinks rather than eat. She is aware that this cycle of drinking to feel better about herself can only lead to serious life problems, but she doesn't think she's capable of stopping. A number of women in the community are secret drinkers, she tells the counselor, and for many of them, drinking is one of the few pleasures they have. Life has stopped having meaning and, faced with many years of living alone and doing nothing, she finds solace in alcohol.

Her counselor has seen the same pattern in older adult alcoholics and has allowed for the fact that the problem will take much longer to resolve because Wanda lacks a support group. The therapist thought that an older adult support group of problem drinkers at the retirement community would help Wanda, but learned from Wanda that all the members have continued drinking and have even formed a club of sorts to drink together.

During one session several months into treatment, the counselor admitted to Wanda that the treatment wasn't helping Wanda with her drinking. While Wanda read articles and came prepared to discuss them, it was an intellectual exercise, and it wasn't helping Wanda change her behavior. Wanda pleaded with the counselor not to give up on her. She was the only person in Wanda's life with whom Wanda could talk. She didn't know what she would do if the counselor gave up on her, and she had openly considered suicide as an option.

The session was electric, as Wanda spoke of her early life and her co-dependency and how it had made relationships impossible. She had lied about her drinking and had a pattern of binge drinking from early adolescence, but had never done anything about it. She thought of herself as a tough-minded woman who had lapses, only this relapse wasn't going away. She promised to "hunker down" and get to work, and she did. On her 70th birthday, she passed six months of sobriety and had her cart privileges returned. With the counselor's recommendation, she also got her driver's license back. She has joined a real estate firm selling re-sales in the retirement community and is busier than ever. And she has found a man her age whom she considers her best friend and companion. In the time she has available after work, they take advantage of the many cultural events in the community. During the hottest months of the summer, they go to the mountains. Little happens during those months at work. If someone contacts the agency, she can handle it on the Internet and by phone.

Wanda's counselor told us, "I'm never surprised when people tell me that they have a history of drinking even though they deny it early in treatment. I wonder about late-onset alcoholism, and, while I'm sure it exists, many older people with no actual history of drinking problems find alcohol aversive both in taste and in its effect. I think Wanda is one of many tough-minded successful women in our society who fill their lives so full that when they take a break and try and relax, many emotional issues come up that they'd rather not deal with. So they work hard, have lots of acquaintances, and stay very busy. When they retire, many years of denial and ignoring problems begin to have an impact. The fact that Wanda read the articles I suggested and came prepared to discuss them gave her a large body of information. When she was ready to begin changing, the material she read came in very handy."

Her counselor continued to say, "I don't want to define Wanda as a success story. Alcohol isn't her only problem. When she becomes too tired to work or fill up her time with other activities, it wouldn't surprise me if she had a relapse. Right now, she's had a scare and she's very motivated. I've referred her for counseling to help her understand the impact of her early life, but she's put it off. I suspect she's had some very bad traumas and maybe she can avoid discussing them but I think sooner or later they'll come back to haunt her."

■ Summary

This chapter deals with the serious problem of substance abuse among older men and women. A number of physical problems have their origins in heavy alcohol use, but physicians often neglect to find out about drinking and therefore treat the physical problem and not the underlying problem of alcohol abuse. The chapter discusses treatment issues with substance abuse including brief treatment, natural healing, and self-help groups. A case study describes an older retired woman experiencing serious alcohol problems, and the counseling she receives to control her drinking after suffering from a serious alcohol-related accident.

▨ Useful Web Sites

About.com: alcoholism. Pain killer abuse increasing among older adults. 2008. http://alcoholism.about.com/od/prescription/a/older_pain.htm

Alcohol Abuse Screening Quiz. 2008. http://alcoholism.about.com/od/problem/a/blquiz1.htm

Gfroerer, Joseph, Michael Penne, Michael Pemberton, and Ralph Folsom. 2003. Substance abuse treatment need among older adults in 2020: the impact of the aging baby-boom cohort. Drug and Alcohol Dependence 69 (2003) 127_/135 https://medicine.johnstrogerhospital.org/cru/images/education/519cd99e959493c0c6ad6bf40b928794.pdf

Medicinenet.com. 2008. Alcoholism. http://www.medicinenet.com/alcohol_abuse_and_alcoholism/article.htm

National Council on Alcoholism and Drug Dependence. 2008. Substance abuse symptom checklist. http://www.ncadd-sfv.org/symptoms/symptom_checklist.html

▨ References

Adams, W. L., K. L. Barry, and M. F. Fleming. 1996. "Screening for problem drinking in older primary care patients." *Journal of the American Medical Association* 276(24): pp. 70–71.

American Psychiatric Association. *Diagnostic and Statistical Manual of Mental Disorders, Fourth Edition*. Washington, DC: American Psychiatric Publishing Company, Inc., 2000.

Atkinson, R. 1995. "Treatment programs for aging alcoholics." In *Alcohol and Aging*, eds. T. Beresford and E. Gomberg, 186–210. New York: Oxford University Press.

Babor, T. F. and J. C. Higgins-Biddle. May 2000. "Alcohol screening and brief intervention: Dissemination strategies for medical practice and public health." *Addiction* 95(5): 677–87.

Barrick, C., and G. J. Connors. 2002. "Relapse prevention and maintaining abstinence in older adults with alcohol-use disorders." *Drugs and Aging* 19:583–94.

Bien, T. J., W. R. Miller, and J. S. Tonigan. 1993. "Brief interventions for alcohol problems: A review." *Addictions* 88(3): 315–35.

Biernacki, P. *Pathways from Heroin Addiction: Recover without Treatment*. Philadelphia: Temple University Press, 1986.

Bisson, J., L. Nadeau, and A. Demers. May 1999. "The validity of the CAGE scale to screen heavy drinking and drinking problems in a general population." *Addiction* 94(5): 15–23.

Blow, F. C. 2007. "Substance abuse among older adults: Treatment improvement protocol (TIP) series 26." *Substance Abuse and Mental Health Services Administration*. http://ncadi.samhsa.gov/govpubs/BKD250/ (accessed on November 17, 2007).

Burge, S. K., N. Amodei, B. Elkin, S. Catala, S. R. Andrew, P. A. Lane, and J. P. Seale. 1997. "An evaluation of two primary care interventions for alcohol abuse among Mexican-American patients." *Addiction* 92(12): 1705–16.

Chang, G., L. Wilkins-Haug, S. Berman, and M. A. Goetz. 1999. "Brief intervention for alcohol use in pregnancy: A randomized trial." *Addiction* 94(10): 1499–1508.

Fleming, M., and L. B. Manwell. 1998. "Brief intervention in primary care settings: A primary treatment method for at-risk, problem, and dependent drinkers." *Alcohol Research and Health* 23(2): 128–37.

Fleming, M. F., K. L. Barry, L. B. Manwell, K. Johnson, and R. London. 1997. "Brief physician advice for problem alcohol drinkers: A randomized controlled trial in community-based primary care practices." *Journal of the American Medical Association* 277(13): 1039–45.

Gentilello, L. M., and D. M. Donovan, C. W. Dunn, and F. P. Rivara. 1995. "Alcohol interventions in trauma centers: Current practice and future directions." *Journal of the American Medical Association* 274(13): 1043–48.

Granfield, R., and W. Cloud. Winter 1996. "The elephant that no one sees: Natural recovery among middle-class addicts." *Journal of Drug Issues* 26:45–61.

Herman, M. (2000). "Psychotherapy with substance abusers: Integration of psychodynamic and cognitive-behavioral approaches." *American Journal of Psychotherapy* 54(4): 574–79.

Higgins-Biddle, J. C., T. F. Babor, J. Mullahy, J. Daniels, and B. McRee. 1997. "Alcohol screening and brief interventions: Where research meets practice." *Connecticut Medicine* 61:565–75.

Hingson, R., N. Scotch, N. Day, and A. Culbert. 1980. "Recognizing and seeking help for drinking problems." *Journal of Studies on Alcohol* 41:1102–17.

Humphreys, K. Winte 1998. "Can addiction-related self-help/mutual aid groups lower demand for professional substance abuse treatment?" *Social Policy* 29(2):13–17.

Liberto, J. G., and D. W. Oslin. 1995. "Early versus late onset of alcoholism in the elderly." *International Journal of Addiction* 30(13–14): 1799–1818.

Menninger, J. A. (2002, Spring). "Source Assessment and treatment of alcoholism and substance-related disorders in the elderly." *Bulletin of the Menninger Clinic* 66(2): 166–84 A.

Miller, K. E. 2001. "Can two questions screen for alcohol and substance abuse?" *American Family Physician* 64: 1247.

Miller, W. R., and S. Rollnick. *Motivational interviewing: Preparing people for change.* New York: Guilford Press, 1991.

Miller, W. R., and V. C. Sanchez. "Motivating young adults for treatment and lifestyle change." In *Alcohol Use and Misuse by Young Adults*, eds. G. S. Howard and P. E. Nathan, 55–81. Notre Dame, IN: University of Notre Dame Press, 1994.

Mukamal, K. J., M. A. Mittleman, W. T. Longstreth, A. B. Newman, L. P. Fried, and D. S. Siscovick. 2004. "Self-reports alcohol consumption and falls in older adults: Cross-sectional and longitudinal analyses of the cardiovascular health study." *Journal of the American Geriatrics Society* 52:1174–79.

National Institute for Alcohol Abuse and Alcoholism, Department of Health and Human Services, Alcohol and Health. *Ninth Special Report to the United States on Alcohol and Health* (NIH Publication No. 97-4017). Washington, DC: U.S. Government Printing Office, 1997.

Onder, G., E. Landi, C. Delia Vedova, H. Atkinson, C. Pedone, M. Cesari, et al. 2002. "Moderate alcohol consumption and adverse drug reactions among older adults." *Pharmacoepidemiological Drug Safety* 11:385–92.

Oslin, D. W. 2004. "Late-life alcoholism: Issues relevant to the geriatric psychiatrist." *American Journal of Geriatric Psychiatry* 12:571–83.

Peele, S. *The diseasing of America: Addiction treatment out of control.* Lexington, MA: Lexington Books, 1989.

Roizen, R., D. Calahan, E. Lambert, W. Wiebel, and P. Shanks. "Spontaneous remission among untreated problem drinkers." In *Longitudinal Research on Drug Use,* ed. D. Kandel, Washington, D.C.: Hemisphere Publishing, 1978.

Seligman, M. E. P. 1995. "The effectiveness of psychotherapy: The consumers report study." *American Psychologist* 50(12): 965–74.

Snow, M. 1973. "Maturing out of narcotic addiction in New York City." *International Journal of the Addictions* 8(6): 932–38.

Sobell, L., M. Sobell, T. Toneatto, and G. Leo. 1993. "What triggers the resolution of alcohol problems without treatment?" *Alcoholism: Clinical and Experimental Research* 17(2): 217–24.

Stall, R., and P. Biernacki. 1989. "Spontaneous remission from the problematic use of substances." *International Journal of the Addictions* 21:1–23.

Stewart, K. B., and A. B. Richards. 2000. "Recognizing and managing your patient's alcohol abuse." *Nursing* 30(2): 56–60.

Substance Abuse and Mental Health Services Administration. 1998. *Substance abuse among older adults: Treatment improvement protocol* (TIP; Series #26). Rockville, MD: U.S. Department of Health and Human Services.

Substance Abuse and Mental Health Services Administration. National Survey on Drug Use and Health. 2004. http:///www.oas.samhsa.gov/nhsda/2k2nsduh/results/2k2Results.htm (accessed August 15, 2008).

Trice, H., and P. Roman. 1970. "Delabeling, relabeling, and Alcoholics Anonymous." *Social Problems* 17:538–46.

Waldorf, D., C. Reinarman, and S. Murphy. *Cocaine changes: The experience of using and quitting.* Philadelphia: Temple University Press, 1991.

Winick, C. 1962. "Maturing out of narcotic addiction." *Bulletin on Narcotics* 6(1): 46–57.

20 ■ ■ ■

The Road Less Traveled

In this book on retirement we've attempted to prepare you for the new, but often very satisfying, world of retirement, a world that offers you a great deal of independence to take the road you've wanted to take during your working and parenting time. We call it "the road less traveled" because it offers you so much opportunity to do many things you weren't able to do earlier in your life. Perhaps another way to word this is "achieving your dreams."

We think you'll be surprised at the many events and opportunities available to you in the community that are affordable, entertaining, and help you grow as a person. In fact, the best thing about retirement is that you'll have the time to think about who you are and the type of person you want to be as you gracefully age. Did you want to write or paint or become an entrepreneur when you were working full-time and raising a family, but just didn't have the time or energy? Now you can do it. Do you want to run for political office or become a board member of a charitable organization? There's nothing stopping you. In fact, you'll be surprised how happy people are to have you volunteer.

Have you been unlucky in love and long for the right person, or what Jewish people call "your *beshert*," your chosen one? Then this is the time to start looking for that person. But you have to put aside your prejudices and look in places you may not have looked before because of your own personal biases. Places of worship are better places to meet singles than clubs. Do you have a problem with going to a place of worship? Just as easily as you can talk yourself into beliefs, you can talk yourself out of them. Do you only want to date women or men who are 20 years younger than you? Then good luck, because your population of eligible singles will be very small. Do you think that only educated people are worth dating? There are wonderful people out there who are smart, funny, and sensitive, but who may not have been able to go to college for a number of practical reasons, but they read and think and long for love, just like you do.

Pessimism is everything it's cracked up to be. If you want to look at things negatively and assume that nothing will work, the chances are that they won't. Self-fulfilling prophecies usually turn out as we expect them to. You can just as easily be optimistic and recognize that you have plenty of time to test the waters, but if you take a chance and it doesn't work out, take it again until it does work out.

This isn't pop psychology or psychobabble. There is considerable research to show that people who are optimistic live longer, handle stress better, are physically healthier, and are much more satisfied with life. The road less traveled takes courage and perseverance. It means changing some negative and pesky attitudes and beliefs.

■ Older Adults Make Important Contributions

We think America needs its older people. There is work to be done in our government, in our charitable organizations, in our places of worship, in our schools, and in every avenue of American life. We think you should take part in helping our country at a time of national difficulty. You can do it by mentoring children who are taking a wrong turn in life and offering support to older people with few resources or friends. You can use your expertise to help others and to help make government work the way it should. Our democracy is based on the notion of a citizen government, not one run by a political class or by bureaucrats.

No one ever said that older people should tune out of life and just play golf and cards for the next 30 years. You have a long life ahead of you. Make the most of it. We have a core of friends in their 70s and 80s who play tennis. One is on the board of Sun City, Arizona. Another continues to build houses. Yet another continues to run his successful insurance company. Another is on the city council, and another drives for meals on wheels. We don't know of anyone who's retired who doesn't take an active role in the civic and business life of our community. Many have had heart problems, but they continue to be active. Some have battled cancer, but they're out on the tennis court and in the community most days. These are the ordinary older people of America, and they continue to live rich lives full of activity and energy.

Having good friends who are positive in the way they view life is vital to happiness in retirement. If you have people around you who always focus on the negatives or tell you why you can't follow the road less traveled, you need to make adjustments in how much time you spend with them, what you talk to them about, and how seriously you take them. Most of us can "tune out" things we don't want to hear. You can do it too with friends and family who are negative and intrude on your dreams.

We have a friend who was president of a large community college and wanted to go to the magical city of Machu Picchu in the Peruvian Andes. During her trip she was riding a horse that bucked her off and she broke her femur. For the next couple of days, she rode back roads and had people she didn't know minister to her pain until she finally had surgery in Lima, Peru, and then flew home. She endured several additional surgeries. Would she do it again? Absolutely! Why? Because it was a dream and she felt compelled to follow it. When she talks about her trip she almost never mentions the accident, but instead her eyes mist over as she talks about the Andes, and the wonderful people, and how she saw the city in the mist, and as the mist lifted how she saw the most marvelous sight she had ever seen. Did she have people tell her how crazy it was to ride horses in the Andes? By the droves. Did she care? Not a bit. She had seen a sight that would never leave her, and she'd had experiences one thinks about forever. At age 70, that's saying a lot.

The economy will have a great deal to do with how you approach retirement. We're optimistic about the health of the economy, but we're concerned that not enough people approaching retirement have saved enough or have planned early enough for their financial futures. We think increasing energy and food costs are likely to be part of the overall picture in America for some time to come. It's vital that you spend time with people who understand finances, work out a financial game plan, and stick with it. Many of us only begin to recognize the need for wise financial advice later in life. Perhaps that's because we are more aware of retirement, and are more settled financially and emotionally to do what needs to be done to have a secure retirement. In any event, saving, wise advice, and a financial game plan are especially important in an era of increasing costs and decreasing pension plans.

■ New Opportunities

We think retirement brings with it many joys, but there are obstacles as well. The initial period after you retire is called the honeymoon period for a good reason. That's the time you feel relieved not to be working and giddy over the freedom you feel, but many people begin to experience that sinking feeling that they don't have enough to do and time begins to go very slowly. We've suggested that you use extended vacations and leaves of absence to test yourself on how well you deal with free time. If it's difficult, then hopefully you will detach yourself from work slowly and incrementally and you'll have a firmed-up plan to cycle into activities that keep you busy when you retire.

Finally, the road less traveled is an opportunity for you to broaden your horizons intellectually. Retirement is not a time to close oneself off from learning. There are many adult-learning programs at local colleges and universities. For those of you who want to go on and get a degree or a different degree from the one you have now, many universities and colleges offer reduced tuition to older adults. Education in America is one of the great bargains. It's inexpensive and it's good. Take the opportunity to broaden your intellectual horizons. Keeping your mind active intellectually is one of the best ways that we know of to stay healthy. Too many retirees lock themselves into a rigid mindset of not wanting to know other sides of arguments or new ways of thinking. "I'm too old and too set in my ways to learn anything new or change my opinions" is just another way of saying, "I don't want to because it makes me work a little." Intellectually rigid people do badly when crises hit because they are ill prepared to handle new situations and new conditions. This goes for all of us, even those of us who have advanced degrees. Learning for the sake of learning is stimulating, and knowledge, for certain, is power.

We want to take this opportunity to thank you for reading our book. We hope that from our book you've gained confidence to meet the challenges but also reap the rewards of retired life. We plan to offer interactive and onsite seminars to help you as you move into retirement. You can find out more about our seminars by going to morleyglicken.com and haascap. com, our respective Web sites. We look forward to meeting you online and in person.

Index

AARP. *See also* American Association of Retired Persons
achievement level, 3
AD. *See also* Alzheimer's disease
adjustment to retirement, 17
adult-learning programs, 187–188
aging, 9, 145–147
alcohol consumption, 170–171; case example, 177–180; identifying abusers, 171–172; recovery without counseling, 175–176; related medical problems, 171; self-help groups, 176–177; short-term treatment, 173–175
Alcoholics Anonymous (AA), 173, 175
AIG Insurance, 54
Alzheimer's disease (AD), 8, 147–149; brain-fitness exercise, 147; computer games, 147; dementia symptoms, 147, 148; diet,

147–148, 149; physical exercise, 148; self-directed personality, 148
American Association of Retired Persons (AARP), 6, 70, 165
annuity, 53–54, 56–57, 58, 65–66, 76, 77
aspirin, in heart health, 152
assets, 30, 34; allocation, 86–87; estate planning, 101–103; estimation, 57–58, 62–63; probate, 101; self-management, 82–83; trusts, 102. *See also* housing
attitudes, toward retirement, 3–4; ratings, 9–10
autistic activities, 6

bankruptcies, 6, 71
bonds, as investment risk reducers, 86
bridge jobs, 18–20
brief intervention, 173–175

About the Authors

MORLEY D. GLICKEN is the former Dean of the Worden School of Social Service in San Antonio, the founding director of the Master of Social Work Department at California State University, San Bernardino, the past Director of the Master of Social Work Program at the University of Alabama, and the former Executive Director of Jewish Family Service of Greater Tucson. He holds a Doctorate in Social Work from the University of Utah. The author of *Evidence Based Practice with Older Adults: A Psychosocial Perspective* and *Evidence Based Practice with Troubled Children and Adolescents*, among other titles, Dr. Glicken has written extensively for the Dow Jones publication *National Business Employment Weekly*. He is currently on the faculty at Arizona State University and is Director of the Institute for Positive Growth: A Research, Treatment, and Training Institute in Prescott, Arizona, that specializes in services to older Americans (www.morleyglicken.com).

BRIAN HAAS is the President and Portfolio Manager for Haas Capital Management, LLC, an Arizona-based Registered Investment Advisor (www.haascap.com). Mr. Haas has over a decade of investment experience and specializes in low-volatility portfolio strategies. Haas Capital Management, LLC provides investment management solutions to affluent and high net worth individuals.